BECOMING A CHRISTIAN

Becoming a Christian

Timothy VonWald

Becoming a Christian
Copyright © 2020 by Timothy VonWald.
All rights reserved.

Unless otherwise indicated, all Scripture quotations are taken from the *Holy Bible,* New Living Translation, copyright © 1996, 2004. Used by permission of Tyndale House Publisher, Inc., Carol Stream, Illinois 60188. All rights reserved.

Scripture quotations marked (ESV) are from The Holy Bible, English Standard Version, copyright © 2001 by Crossway Bibles, a division of Good News Publishers. Used by permission. All rights reserved.

Scripture quotations marked (TEV) are from The Holy Bible, Today's English Version, copyright © 1992 by American Bible Society, New York. Used by permission.

Definitions of Biblical words were referenced with Strong's Exhaustive Concordance of the Bible. Written by James Strong. Published by Hendrickson Publishers. No copyright listed.

Strong's numbers used in citations (Strong's Hebrew #) and (Strong's Greek #) refer to the entry numbers for each word listed in the Hebrew and Greek dictionaries of the Strong's Exhaustive Concordance of the Bible.

Format used for scripture citations is listed in Resource 2: Bible Tools, II. Finding Scriptures.

Published by Spiritfire Publishing, LLC
www.spiritfirepublishing.com

ISBN: 978-0-9972078-4-2
REL012000: Religion / Christian Living / General
REL012120: Religion / Christian Living / Spiritual Growth
REL012070: Religion / Christian Living / Personal Growth

Dedication

This book is dedicated to:

God, Our Heavenly Father,

Jesus Christ, Our Lord and Savior,

The Reader, God's cherished treasure.

Table of Contents

Introduction 9
Unit 1: The Good News 15
    Lesson 1: Where did I Come From? 17
    Lesson 2: How Do I Become Saved? 27
    Lesson 3: Where Are We Going? 37
Unit 2: God 47
    Lesson 1: Who is God? 49
    Lesson 2: Who is Jesus Christ? 57
    Lesson 3: What is God Like? 69
Unit 3: Devotions 79
    Lesson 1: Prayer 81
    Lesson 2: Bible 93
    Lesson 3: Praise 103
Unit 4: The Church 111
    Lesson 1: God's Family 113
    Lesson 2: Baptism and The Lord's Supper 123
    Lesson 3: Giving and Service 135
Unit 5: Sanctification 147
    Lesson 1: The Sinful Nature 149
    Lesson 2: Following the Holy Spirit 159
    Lesson 3: Personal Convictions 169

Unit 6: Spiritual Warfare 179
    Lesson 1: The Enemy 181
    Lesson 2: The Devil's Schemes 193
    Lesson 3: God's Mighty Champions! 205

Unit 7: Christian Living 215
    Lesson 1: Witnessing 217
    Lesson 2: Christians at Work 229
    Lesson 3: Christians in Society 239

Epilogue: The Race 249

Resources 253
    Resource 1: Reviewing 255
    Resource 2: Bible Tools 273
    Resource 3: Church Tools 285

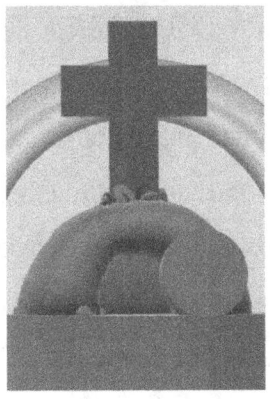

INTRODUCTION

Why did I write this book?

I love the thought of leading people to Christ. Christians who specialize in getting people saved are truly a gift from God. I thank God for them. I believe it's great that churches have Christians going door to door, leading others to Jesus Christ.

However, I have also noticed that some churches tend to neglect these new Christians after they get saved. They get so busy reaching out to new people that they forget the people they have already reached out to.

These new Christians have no one to teach them about God. So, they quickly drift off, going back into the sinful lifestyle they were supposed to leave behind.

Jesus talked about this tendency for new Christians to drift back into sin in Matthew 13:1-9, 18-23. He compared the people who hear the Good News to different types of soil that the seed of the Good News is planted into. Some people never receive the Good News. As soon as they hear it, they refuse to believe it. Others are like the seeds planted on the rocky ground or the weedy ground. There, God's word settles and grows for a little while, but then some form of hardship or distraction takes it away from them. Other people are like the good ground who accept God's word and retain it until they reach spiritual maturity.

The point is, getting people saved is important, but it is not enough. It's just as important to keep Christians saved and to help them grow up to spiritual maturity. Developing spiritual maturity takes time.

In the same way that a child needs time to grow up, a new Christian needs time to mature. I wrote this book specifically to give new Christians a starting point to reach spiritual maturity. I will try to teach you good Christian habits, which also take some time to develop. But Jesus Christ is with you at all times and with him there is nothing you cannot do (Matthew 28:20; Philippians 4:13).

Who am I writing to?

The people who I am writing this for are new Christians, particularly those who are teenagers or adults. You may have been young or old when you decided to come to Jesus Christ for salvation, but that doesn't matter. If you were at any time in the last year or two converted to Christ, I am writing to you.

That is why I am also trying to write as simply and clearly as possible, because I know not everyone enjoys theological terms. When I do introduce a church-related word, I try to give it a clear explanation.

What do I hope to accomplish?

I hope to give you a basic understanding of the most commonly held teachings of Christianity. I'm not going to attempt to tell you everything there is to know about Christianity. That would take several volumes to write about. But what I will show you is enough information for you to begin to discover things for yourself.

For example, in the lesson on the Bible, instead of trying to tell you everything I know about the Bible, I simply give you a plan for reading, studying or memorizing from the Bible. In other words, I don't try to tell you everything, but I show you where to go to find the answers.

I have also included a Resources Section at the back of the book to help you find tools and answers you need.

By the time you are done reading this book, you should be able to develop a basic pattern of prayer and Bible reading.

How do I hope to get you there?

When writing this book, I often use the Question and Answer format, because it tends to work so well. Let me illustrate. In what year did Christopher Columbus discover the New World?

You probably already know the answer to this question without me saying anything. But it is the question that jogs your memory and makes you think.

When I was in middle school and high school, I quickly discovered that the teachers I enjoyed the most were not the ones who dumped a bunch of information on me to memorize like some parrot. The teachers I liked the most were the ones who challenged me, who prodded my mind with questions which I had to figure out answers to. So, when you see a question in this book, don't just read on to the next sentence. Pause for a second and ask yourself what you think the answer is and why.

The second way that I hope to help you get there is by asking review questions which can be rehearsed over and over again. At the end of each lesson there is a review section. Please don't skip over it. Take some time to review them.

At the end of the book is a large review section which covers the entire book. This is for long-term reviewing. You can't possibly remember something important by reviewing it only once. You have to review it over and over until you can quote it in your sleep. That is one of the ways people learn.

Another way people learn is by practical application, which is why I have included sections on Application and Prayer, so that you can practice what you have just been taught. It's not enough just to know something. You must also apply what you know. You must act out what you believe.

By the time you are done reading this book, you should know what you need to do next. You should be able to come up with a plan for reading the Bible and prayer. You should have a home church that you can go to. You should be beginning to live the sanctified life.

What do I need from you?

The two biggest things that I need from you are time and a willingness to learn.

If you have been living in sin all your life, please don't expect God to transform you into a perfect saint overnight. For many people, lasting change takes time. God can change you into a perfect Christian overnight, but He often doesn't. That is because learning patience is part of the process.

Yes, learning through patience is more difficult than having God simply hand holiness over to us, but a large part of Christianity is learning to trust in God (Hebrews 11:6). And we can't truly learn to trust God without having some difficulties or challenges.

The other thing I need from you is a willingness to learn. If you believe you know everything, how can you possibly learn anything? Having a willingness to learn means choosing humility over pride. It means paying attention to what you are reading instead of mentally tuning out, doubting or criticizing the author.

Learning to live as a Christian is like learning any other discipline. You only get out of it what you put into it.

UNIT 1: THE GOOD NEWS

According to 1 Corinthians 15, the Good News is the death, burial and resurrection of Jesus Christ. Jesus Christ died for our sins by being nailed to a cross. He was buried in a tomb. Later, He rose again so that we could live a new life in Him.

But why did Jesus need to die in the first place? What does that make us (Christians) now? What will happen to us when we die? In Unit 1: The Good News, I will try to answer these and other questions.

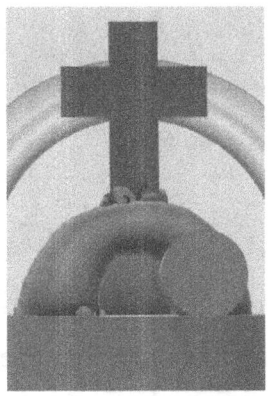

Lesson 1: Where Did I Come From?

Today we will learn how to answer the following questions:

1. How did God create people?
2. How does God view humanity today?
3. What is the punishment for sin?
4. What is the Good News?

1. How Did God Create Humans?

Genesis chapter one tells us how God made the world we live in. On one day God made light. On another day he made the plants. On another day God made birds and fish. On another day God made people.

How did God originally make people?

So God created human beings in his own image. In the image of God he created them; male and female he created them.
Genesis 1:27 (NLT)

When God first made **people**, we **were good**, literally. (Genesis 1:31) We were made in God's image. We were morally perfect, just like God is perfect. God gave us rule over the earth (Genesis 1:28). We tended to think and act humbly and fairly and kindly, just like God. We were, in fact, God's representation on the earth.

God made people good.

Something happened which wiped away this early paradise. Can you guess what it was?

2. How Does God View Humanity Today?

Genesis 2-3 gives us the account of the first people (Adam and Eve) and how their one act of disobedience made all people slaves to sin. First God gave them a command—you may eat fruit from any tree in the garden except the Tree of Knowledge of Good and Evil (Genesis 2:16-17).

Later on (we don't know how much later), a snake came along and tricked Eve into eating the forbidden fruit. She disobeyed God and then she persuaded Adam to disobey God, too.

In this way, Adam and Eve brought sin to all people, because the fact of the matter is this: every person sins (Romans 5:12).

You don't have to look far to find examples of sinning. All you have to do is open a newspaper and read about who killed whom or who robbed whom. The fact

All people have sinned.

that we even have a system of courts and judges testifies to the fact that we know some things are evil and yet, we keep on choosing to do evil, instead of good.

Otherwise, if we did not know some things were evil, how could we punish anybody for a crime? If we really were good people, then why would we need police officers and judges to enforce laws?

The sad truth is, from Genesis 3 to the end of the Bible, God no longer calls all people good (Revelation 22:11)
.

3. What is the Punishment for Sin?

But the Lord God warned him (Adam), "You may freely eat the fruit of every tree in the garden -- except the tree of the knowledge of good and evil. If you eat its fruit, you are sure to die."
Genesis 2:16-17 (NLT)

What is the punishment for sin?

It is death. If we sin, we are sure to die. It is stated again in Romans 6:23:

For the wages of sin is death, but the free gift of God is eternal life through Christ Jesus our Lord.
(NLT)

Sin kills people. Sometime after Adam and Eve sinned, God spoke to them and asked them why they sinned. Then he pronounced several curses upon Adam and Eve, the chief curse being, death.

All people will die, because of sin.

All people die. There is no one born into this world who does not die, eventually.

But as Christians, we need to remember that the punishment for sin is even more severe than that. What happens to an evil person after he or she dies?

I saw the dead, both great and small, standing before God's throne. And the books were opened, including the Book of Life. And the dead were judged according to what they had done, as recorded in the books...Then death and the grave were thrown into the lake of fire. This lake of fire is the second death. And anyone whose name was not found recorded in the Book of Life was thrown into the lake of fire.
Revelation 20:12, 14-15 (NLT)

The first death is only temporary, but the second death lasts forever. It is a form of pain and suffering which never has an end. Jesus described it as the place where worms do not die and the fire is never put out (Mark 9:48).

4. What is the Good News?

God could have left us to our fate. He could have said, "Well, I gave those people a chance to do good and they failed. So, I'm going to wipe out the entire human race and start over." God would have been perfectly just in doing so. In fact, he nearly did wipe out all people with a huge flood in Genesis 6.

But God isn't only just. He is also kind. It was God's kindness which caused him to spare humanity from the flood. It was also God's kindness, which caused him to send his only Son, Jesus Christ, into our sinful world.

Jesus Christ did the one thing we could not do. He lived a life without sin, a life pleasing to God (Matthew 3:16-17; Hebrews 4:14-15). Then Jesus took the punishment which was meant for us (2 Corinthians 5:21). Jesus died for us so that we would not have to suffer the second death.

Jesus was nailed to a wooden cross. He died, was buried and in three days rose again. In effect, Jesus gave us a new life apart from sin,

Jesus died and came back to life to save us from sin.

which guarantees our salvation from the Lake of Fire. **The story of Jesus' death and resurrection** is what we call the Good News (1 Corinthians 15:1-8).

It's called the Good News, because it is what makes us good people. The Good News brings us back into a right relationship with God.

Review

Let's see how much of this lesson you remember. You can find the answers in the lesson above or in the Answers Section of the Resources in the back of this book.

1. How did God create humanity?

2. What is God's view of humanity, today?

3. What is the punishment for sin? (Two things)

4. What is the Good News?

Application

The whole point of God's conviction is to help us to face the truth about ourselves. Without God's help, we are evil people. But the first step towards getting saved is admitting that you are an evil person. There's nothing God can do for you, if you are constantly lying to him about how good you are.

So, I want to ask you, "Have you talked to God about your sins?" If you haven't, then now is a good time to start. You can begin by talking to God about your sins and asking him to forgive you.

Prayer Time

Lesson 2: How Do I Become Saved?

Today, you will learn to answer the following questions:

1. How do I become saved?
2. What does God do to save us?
3. What is becoming a Christian like?
4. What are the benefits of becoming a Christian?

1. How do we receive salvation?

If you confess with your mouth that Jesus is Lord and believe in your heart that God raised him from the dead, you will be saved.
Romans 10:9 (NLT)

To confess that Jesus is Lord means more than just saying he is a lord among other lords. Rather, Jesus is sovereign (Strong's Greek 2962). He is above all others. He is even over you. This is perhaps the hardest part of Christianity: letting go of yourself. You can't be the boss of your life anymore. Jesus is the boss of you, if you truly believe Jesus is Lord.

Receiving salvation isn't difficult or complicated. If you want God to save you, you simply ask for it. That is all. God doesn't require you to climb the highest mountain or swim to the bottom of the sea. He only asks you to **confess and believe**. That is all.

> *Confess Jesus is Lord.*
> *Believe God raised him from the dead.*

2. How does God save us from sin?

God saved you by his grace when you believed. And you can't take credit for this; it is a gift from God. Salvation is not a reward for the good things we have done, so none of us can boast about it.
Ephesians 2:8-9 (NLT)

Notice the way God saves us from our sins. We didn't earn it. We could do nothing to make salvation our right, because apart from Christ we are really sinners. It's only Christ who saves us. There is nothing we can do to save ourselves.

It's easy for professing Christians to get caught up in good works, as if they owe God some massive debt to get paid off. It's like begging God for a car, when you already have one sitting in your driveway. If God has given you salvation, why are you working so hard to get it?

The reason why many people want to earn salvation is so they can boast about it. They want to prove that they are better than the next guy. The truth is, none of us are good without Christ. Only trusting Jesus Christ can make us good.

We are saved by God's grace.

Please notice that I'm not saying Christians shouldn't do good works. Just the opposite. One of the signs of mature Christians is that they are full of good works (James 2:17). But mature Christians don't do good works to earn salvation. They do good works because they love God.

3. What is becoming a Christian like?

This means that anyone who belongs to Christ has become a new person. The old life is gone; a new life has begun!
2 Corinthians 5:17 (NLT)

Have you ever wanted the opportunity to start over again? That's the best part of becoming a Christian. It is the chance to start over again. You had a life which you squandered living mostly for yourself. You lived under the oppressive slavery of sin's rule and were helpless to change.

Any person who knows about addictions knows how very hard it is to stop sinning. People who get caught up in sins of drugs and alcohol abuse know how hard it is to stop. It's also hard to stop lusting, cussing, and coveting as well.

But coming to Christ gives you a fresh start. It's like starting out with a brand new canvas, after the last painting you did was a flop. So, you get a new life when you come to Jesus Christ, after sin ruined the old life you lived.

Becoming a Christian gives you the opportunity to let go of those old vices. This doesn't mean that you'll never sin again and it doesn't mean that getting rid of those old vices will be easy. But it does means that sin no longer controls you. You now have the freedom to walk away from sin. And if you love God, you will walk away from sin.

You are a new person!

But if for some reason you do sin, it doesn't mean that God won't forgive you. Rather, he is simply waiting for you to admit the sin so that he can forgive you (1 John 1:9). It's no benefit to

God to condemn you, not when he already gave his Son, Jesus Christ, to save you (Romans 8:31-33).

4. What are the *benefits* of becoming a Christian?

Therefore, since we have been made right in God's sight by faith, we have peace with God because of what Jesus Christ our Lord has done for us. Because of our faith, Christ has brought us into this place of undeserved privilege where we now stand, and we confidently and joyfully look forward to sharing God's glory.
Romans 5:1-2 (NLT)

When we make Jesus Christ our Lord, we **become righteous** in God's sight. It is as if God is calling you good, just like He called His creation good before people became enslaved to sin. We didn't do anything to earn God's approval. Rather, we received the righteousness of Jesus Christ. It also does not mean that we will never sin, but that we are no longer slaves to sin.

When God calls us "good," a truly wonderful thing happens. We are now at **peace with God.** We are no longer living under condemnation. We don't have to suffer under a troubled conscience anymore, because we are now living to please God. So, God is no longer our enemy. We are no longer at war with God. We have switched sides. We are now on God's team.

Since we are now on God's team, we now have **God's favor.** We have a place in God's kingdom, where God grants us favors. We can ask God to satisfy our needs and trust that He will listen to our prayers.

We can also look forward to a bright future ahead of us. God gives us **eternal life** (John 3:16). We get to live with God forever, sharing in the joy and wealth of His kingdom. This is the biggest reason for people to turn to Christ for salvation. Without eternal life, we have nothing to look forward to, but to suffer forever in the Lake of Fire.

1. *God declares us righteous.*
2. *We have peace with God.*
3. *We have God's favor.*
4. *We have eternal life.*

Trusting in Christ gives us confidence that this condemnation will not be our fate, but that we will live for ever in the glorious presence of God.

Review

In addition to the review questions below, I would like you to try to answer the review questions from the previous lesson. You can find them either at the end of each lesson or in the Review Section in the back of the book.

1. How do we become saved? (Two things)

2. How does God save us from sin?

3. What is becoming a Christian like?

4. What are the benefits of becoming a Christian? (Four things)

Application

Have you made Jesus Christ your Lord and Savior?

If you haven't, now is a good time to start. You might want to say a prayer like this: *Dear God, I am a sinner. I believe the Lord Jesus died and rose again to save me from my sins. So, please forgive me of my sins. Thank you.*

In Luke 15, Jesus told three stories to share with us how God feels about a sinner who turns from his sins to Jesus Christ. God rejoices. He gets excited and happy. It's a wonderful victory, a glorious moment. All of heaven shouts with praise over a sinner who comes to God in repentance. God gladly accepts you as one of his own and you will never ever be turned away. (John 6:37)

Prayer Time

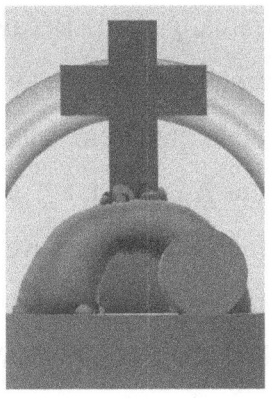

Lesson 3: Where Are We Going?

We already know what happens to unbelievers when they die, but what happens to the Christian? By the time we have completed this lesson, you should be able to answer the following questions.

1. What happens to Christians after they die?
2. Why should Christians live to please God?
3. Where do those who love God ultimately wind up?

1. What happens to Christians after they die?

Just as everyone dies because we all belong to Adam, everyone who belongs to Christ will be given new life. But there is an order to this resurrection: Christ was raised as the first of the harvest; then all who belong to Christ will be raised when he comes back.
    1 Corinthians 15:22-23 (NLT)

Adam sinned and eventually died. Because every person is a descendant of Adam, we all sin and die, too. We were born with a sinful nature, which we inherited from Adam. So we eventually sin and eventually die, just as Adam did.

But when we become Christians, we belong to Jesus Christ. So, we inherit Christ's righteousness. Jesus Christ died on the cross to save us from our sins, but He rose from the grave three days later. Christ took the punishment for our sins to make us righteous.

So, we know we will all one day die, because we sinned. We also know that we will not remain dead. Because we inherit Jesus Christ's righteousness, we also inherit His eternal life. So, we can be confident that we will come back to life, just like Jesus did. **We will come back to life when Jesus Christ returns from heaven.**

By becoming a Christian we not only inherit Christ's righteousness, but also his eternal life. Even though we don't deserve to live for ever, we can, because we belong to Jesus Christ.

That is why I hate to say that a person who loves God is dead, because it is not completely true. A person who loves God might lose his or her body. His or her body might die, temporarily. But if that person is in Christ, that person cannot die, because that person has eternal life. So, instead of dying, we go to be with the Lord (2 Corinthians 5:8).

> *We will come back to life when Jesus returns.*

Jesus told her, "I am the resurrection and the life. Anyone who believes in me will live, even after dying. Everyone who lives in me and believes in me will never ever die."
John 11:25-26a (NLT)

2. Why should Christians live a life to please God?

So now there is no condemnation for those who belong to Christ Jesus.
Romans 8:1 (NLT)

This scripture teaches us that we no longer need to fear eternal condemnation, but we will still be judged.

So whether we are here in this body or away from this body, our goal is to please him. For we must all stand before Christ to be judged. We will each receive whatever we deserve for the good or evil we have done in this earthly body.
2 Corinthians 5:9-10 (NLT)

Sometimes people wonder, "What is the purpose of Christianity? If we don't have to earn our salvation, what are we supposed to be doing?" We are supposed to live to please God. We should live as if our lives really belong to God, because they do.

And we will have to answer to Jesus Christ for everything we do and say, whether we are a Christian or not (Matthew 25:40, 45; 12:36).

Knowing that **Jesus Christ will one day judge us** should not terrify us, because we know we will not be condemned. However, it should make us afraid to sin. If we realize that we cannot cheat God's justice, we will be less likely to do something wrong.

To face Christ's judgment is to simply face the truth (Hebrews 4:13). You don't have to be afraid of the truth, if you are doing what is right. But if we continue to live life only for ourselves, we will likely be ashamed when Jesus Christ returns (1 John 2:28). That's why it is important to live in a way that pleases God.

> *Jesus will judge us.*

3. What happens after we are judged by Jesus Christ?

Then I saw a new heaven and a new earth, for the old heaven and the old earth had disappeared. And the sea was also gone. And I saw the holy city, the new Jerusalem, coming down from God out of heaven like a bride beautifully dressed for her husband. I heard a loud shout from the throne, saying, "Look, God's home is now among his people! He will live with them, and they will be his people. God himself will be with them. He will wipe every tear

from their eyes, and there will be no more death or sorrow or crying or pain. All these things are gone forever."
Revelation 21:1-4 (NLT)

Revelation 21 describes the **new paradise** that God has prepared for you and me. The sorrow of this present life will no longer exist. Everything will be restored back to its rightful place as God intended it.

Jesus said, that those whose hearts are pure will see God (Matthew 5:8). So, the invisible God who we know of today will no longer be invisible. **God will be with us**. We will see his face and talk to him as if we were talking to a friend.

We will have **an eternal home** with him in the New Jerusalem where we will never cry or be sick or suffer pain or hunger or thirst or grieve ever again. This old way of living will be forever dead.

One thing we should always remember as Christians is this. From God's perspective, our lives last only a moment (Isaiah 51:6). We are going to spend a lot more time in eternity with God than we will be suffering here on earth. So, shouldn't we care more about what be happening in eternity than what we are facing in our daily struggles?

We will live in a new paradise, with God in an eternal home.

THE AROMA OF HEAVEN

One of my favorite holidays is Thanksgiving. Everybody gathers around the table to enjoy a great Thanksgiving Day feast. How I love to eat on Thanksgiving! But the hard part about Thanksgiving is the waiting. The Thanksgiving Day feast doesn't begin until everything is cooked and ready.

So, often on Thanksgiving Day my stomach is rumbling. I'll be sitting there talking or watching television, anything to get my mind off of how hungry I am. That's because I'm waiting for something special. I'm waiting for the moment when the cook steps out of the kitchen and announces that the Thanksgiving dinner is ready. Then we can all gather around the table to start eating.

Now, while I'm waiting for this special moment, I usually can't tell what's going on in the kitchen. The kitchen doors are usually closed off. So, I can't really tell exactly which foods are being cooked or served. But I can smell the aroma. It is the aroma which assures my rumbling stomach that as difficult as it is to wait, the dinner will be ready soon and the reward for waiting is well worth it.

The Bible tells us that the Holy Spirit is the foretaste of heaven (Romans 8:23). He is like the aroma of heaven sent to assure us that eternal life is really ours (2 Corinthians 5:5). It was the Holy Spirit who raised Jesus Christ from the dead. It is the Holy Spirit who will raise us from the dead, too. So, we don't need to worry about whether or not our hopes are real. God has a place in His house reserved for you (John 14:2).

Review

In this last lesson of the unit, I would like you to review not only this lesson, but all the previous lessons you have read in this unit. Please try to continue doing this at the end of each unit you complete. You can find a complete list of review questions and answers under Resource 1: Reviewing in the back of the book.

1. What will happen after a Christian dies?

2. Why should Christians live to please God?

3. What does God offer us in eternity? (Three things)

Application

1. How does knowing there is a place in the New Jerusalem waiting for you help you gain victory over struggles in this life?

2. What can you do to focus more upon eternity?

Prayer Time

When you pray, please remember to thank God for saving you and for giving you an eternal home.

UNIT 2: GOD

When we try to understand God, we must keep in mind that we are trying to understand someone who is much greater than we are. For us to understand the concepts of God is a lot like an ant trying to understand the human concept of money.

This doesn't mean that we are clueless when it comes to understanding God. We know about God the things He has revealed to us in the Scriptures. However, there is a certain amount of mystery about God just like a husband can be married to his wife for several years and still find her somewhat mysterious.

So, some of the things we talk about in this unit may seem contradictory, on the surface. I hope you will try to keep an open mind. Thank you.

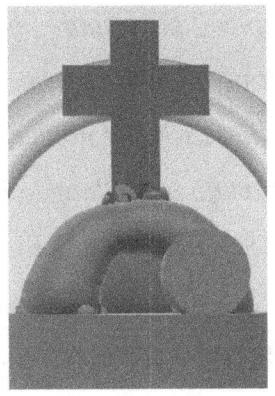

Lesson 1: Who Is God?

1. Who are the three persons in the Godhead?
2. Who is the Father?
3. Who is the Son?
4. Who is the Holy Spirit?

1. Who is the Godhead?

The first question people like to ask about God is, "How many Gods are there?"

> *The LORD is God and there is no other.*
> Deuteronomy 4:35b (NLT)

> *In the beginning the Word already existed. The Word was with God, and the Word was God.*
> John 1:1 (NLT)

But you are not controlled by your sinful nature. You are controlled by the Spirit if you have the Spirit of God living in you. (And remember that those who do not have the Spirit of Christ living in them do not belong to him at all.)
Romans 8:9 (NLT)

Do you notice any apparent contradictions here? In Deuteronomy we read there is only one God. In John we read that there is another person with God who is equal to God. If you keep on reading, you will discover that this divine person who is with God is called God's Son or Son of God (John 1:14). The fact that God has a son suggests that God is a Father (2 Corinthians 11:31).

Then to make things even more complicated, we read in Romans 8:9, that God has a Spirit who is apparently the same as the Spirit of Christ, God's Son. (Mark 1:1) This Spirit appears to be a different person from either Father or Son (John 14:16-17).

So, in answering the question, "How many Gods are there?" the most accurate way I can describe it is this. The Godhead is **one God in three persons: the Father, the Son, and the Holy Spirit.**

One God in three persons: Father, Son and Holy Spirit

Therefore, go and make disciples of all the nations, baptizing them in the name of the Father and the Son and the Holy Spirit.
Matthew 28:19 (NLT)

2. Who is the Father?

> *Pray like this: Our Father in heaven,*
> *may your name be kept holy.*
> Matthew 6:9 (NLT)

Jesus taught his disciples to pray as if talking to a Heavenly Father. Jesus often called God, his Heavenly Father (Matthew 7:21). You might think of the Father as, **God above us**, because He lives and rules in heaven. (Psalms 115:16) He is sovereign, over everything (1 Corinthians 15:27-28). He is also holy; he cannot tolerate sin (Leviticus 11:44). When we pray, we pray to the Father. Although, this does not mean that we cannot talk to Jesus or the Holy Spirit, too.

The Father is God above us.

The Heavenly Father is good and generous (Matthew 7:11). He is merciful and just. He is patient, truthful, and loving. (Exodus 34:6-7)

3. Who is the Son?

> *Christ is the visible image of the invisible God. He existed before*
> *anything was created and is supreme over all creation, for*
> *through him God created everything in the heavenly realms and*
> *on earth.*
> Colossians 1:15-16a (NLT)

Jesus Christ is God's Son (Mark 1:1). He is our Savior and His death, burial and resurrection save us from our sins.

In the same way that the Father can be thought of as God in heaven, Jesus can be thought of as **God with us** (Isaiah 7:14). That is because Jesus Christ lived with us. He became a human being just like us, and walked beside us (John 1:18).

Jesus Christ is also sovereign. He has all authority, just like the Father (Matthew 28:18). However, Jesus Christ is under the Father's authority. The Father delegated His authority to the Son.

Right now, Jesus is in heaven with the Father. But Jesus is still with us in the sense that He is our means to accessing the Father (1 Timothy 2:5). The only way that a holy God will hear the prayers of sinful people is if there is someone in-between. That person is Jesus. Jesus makes us holy so that we can pray to God. That is why we pray in Jesus' name (John 14:13).

> *Jesus is God with us.*

4. Who is the Holy Spirit?

> *All who confess that Jesus is the Son of God have God living in them, and they live in God.*
> 1 John 4:15 (NLT)

> *You received God's Spirit when he adopted you as his own children. Now we call him, "Abba, Father."*
> Romans 8:15b (NLT)

Unlike Jesus, who was a tangible person, the Holy Spirit is intangible. He is like the wind in that He is everywhere and yet you cannot see Him (Psalms 139:7-12).

The Father is God above us, and Jesus Christ is God with us. So the Holy Spirit is **God in us**. This does not mean that we are God. Rather, the Holy Spirit joins us to God just like glue can join one piece of paper to another (Romans 8:16).

Have you ever been prompted to do something good? Have you ever been inspired to be generous to someone who was needy or to tell the truth even when it hurts? Well, if you have, then there is a good chance that was the Holy Spirit who was prompting you.

In fact, it's the Holy Spirit who is driving us to seek God, to become saved, to turn from our old sinful lifestyles, and to do what is right. The Holy Spirit is God in us, working through us to do God's will on earth (Philippians 2:13).

The Holy Spirit is God in us.

Review

1. Who is the Godhead?

2. Who is God, the Father?

3. Who is God, the Son?

4. Who is the Holy Spirit?

Application

When we pray, we pray to God the Father, through Christ the Son, by the help of the Holy Spirit. God is our Heavenly Father. Jesus Christ is our Lord and the Holy Spirit gives us access to God.

1. In which ways does God act towards us like a Father in Heaven?

2. In which ways does God act like a Sovereign Lord over our lives?

Prayer Time

Take a moment and pray to God. Feel free to ask questions from Him about what He is like and how you can get to know Him better. You may feel free to introduce yourself to God as well.

Lesson 2: Who Is Jesus Christ?

1. Who is Jesus Christ?
2. How is Jesus human?
3. How is Jesus divine?
4. What is Jesus doing today?

1. Who is Jesus Christ?

And she will have a son, and you are to name him Jesus, for he will save his people from their sins.
Matthew 1:21 (NLT)

These words were spoken by one of God's angels to Joseph and Mary, the earthly parents of Jesus. The name **Jesus means, "The Lord saved"** (Strong's Greek 2424, Hebrew 3091). It is an appropriate name since it was Jesus' death and resurrection which saved us from our sins.

The name **Christ means "Anointed One"** or Messiah referring to Jesus' role as king. (Isaiah 61:1; John 1:41; Strong's Greek 5547) The primary role of Jesus earthly ministry was bringing the God's Kingdom to us (Matthew 4:17; Luke 17:21).

Jesus Christ is our King and our Savior. He has freed us from being ruled by sin and transferred us to God's rule. In doing so, He saved our souls from sin and gave to us eternal life. But Jesus isn't just called Lord or Christ. Jesus is also known as Son of Man, and Son of God. Perhaps one of the greatest mysteries about Christ is how He can be both human and God (divine).

Jesus means "The Lord saved"
Christ means "Anointed One"

2. In what ways is Jesus human?

For even the Son of Man came not to be served but to serve others and to give his life as a ransom for many.
Matthew 20:28 (NLT)

In Matthew, Mark and Luke, Jesus' most commonly used term for Himself is Son of Man. The term Son of Man, simply means human. If a man had a son, that man's son would also be a man.

As I talked about earlier, Jesus had **parents**. Jesus was **born** into a human body (Luke 2:4-7). Jesus had an **ethnic group**; He was a Jew (John 4:22). He **ate** food and **slept**, just like we do (Matthew 11:19; 8:23-26). Jesus was **tempted** (Luke 4:1-2). Jesus also **died** (Luke 23:46).

The only difference between Jesus and us is that Jesus never sinned (Hebrews 4:14-15). Jesus is the perfect human. He is what God intended humanity to be like.

One of my favorite stories in the Bible is found in Mark 4:35-39. In this story, the disciples are in a fishing boat and they try to cross the Sea of Galilee. But a big storm sneaks up on them and threatens to capsize the boat.

So, what do the disciples do? They panic. They try everything they can think of to keep the boat afloat, because if the boat goes under, so do they. Then they notice Jesus is in the boat with them and can you guess what Jesus is doing? He's sleeping. The disciples are about to drown and Jesus is sleeping.

> *Jesus was born, had parents, had an ethnic group, ate, slept, was tempted and died just like any other human.*

So, they wake Jesus up, still panicking, and Jesus calms the storm. Then he tries to calm the disciples.

Don't think of Jesus as some stoic, historical figure who lived and died a long time ago. He was a real person, just like people today, with real emotions and real physical needs. There were times when Jesus was hungry, times when he was thirsty. There were times when he laughed and times when he cried. There was even one time when a Roman officer surprised Jesus (Matthew 8:10).

3. In what ways is Jesus divine?

In the beginning the Word already existed. The Word was with God, and the Word was God. He existed in the beginning with God. God created everything through him, and nothing was created except through him.
John 1:1-3 (NLT)

So the Word became human and made his home among us. He was full of unfailing love and faithfulness. And we have seen his glory, the glory of the Father's one and only Son.
John 1:14 (NLT)

Jesus is the Son of God (Mark 1:1). Now, if God had a son, that son would also be God. So, even though Jesus is human, he is also God. I know that's a little difficult to understand. So, I ask you to try to keep an open mind.

In what way is Jesus divine?

In the first place, Jesus' existence did not begin with birth and conception. He lived *before* he was born. Jesus has no origin, because **Jesus always existed.** He is eternal just like the Father is eternal (Genesis 1:1). Jesus' birth was actually His entrance into our world, His way of becoming a human, just like us.

Jesus, also **created all things.** Through Jesus everything was created. We don't know exactly what Jesus' role was in creation, but we do know that he was involved in the creation process, just like the Father and the Holy Spirit. (Genesis 1:1-2)

Jesus **claimed to be God.** Jesus did not go around bragging about being God, but he did mention it several times. He mentioned it in response to the questioning from the High Priest (Matthew 26:63-64; Luke 22:70). He mentioned it in the Gospel of John, using the phrase: "I AM," which was the meaning of the most sacred name of God (Exodus 3:13-14).

There are several of these I AM statements in John's Gospel:

- I AM the Bread of Life (John 6:35).
- I AM the Door (John 10:7).
- I AM the Good Shepherd (John 10:11).
- I AM the Resurrection and the Life (John 11:25).
- I AM the Way, the Truth and the Life (John 14:6).
- I AM in the Father and the Father in me (John 14:10).
- I AM the true Vine (John 15:1).
- Before Abraham was, I AM. (John 8:58)

The **many miracles** Jesus performed offer proof that Jesus was who He said he was. Jesus fed 5,000 men, not counting the women and children (Matthew 14:21, Luke 9:14; John 6:10). Jesus healed a woman who could not stop bleeding (Matthew 9:18-22, Mark 5:24-34, Luke 8:43). Jesus walked on water (Matthew 14:24-25, Mark 6:47-48; John 6:19). Jesus restored the dead back to life (Luke 7:11-15; 8:52-55; John 11:43-44). As an insightful blind man once said of Jesus, *"If this man were not from God, he couldn't have done it."* John 9:33 (NLT)

Probably the greatest proof of his divinity is **Jesus' resurrection**. Jesus is the only person who came back to life *under his own power*. (John 10:17-18) I don't know exactly how Jesus raised himself back to life, but I do know that he did it with the help of the Father and the Holy Spirit (Romans 8:11; 10:9).

Jesus always existed, created all things, claimed to be God, performed many miracles and raised himself from the dead.

4. What is Jesus doing today?

"Who then will condemn us? No one—for Christ Jesus died for us and was raised to life for us, and he is sitting in the place of honor at God's right hand, pleading for us."
Romans 8:34 (NLT)

"My dear children, I am writing this to you so that you will not sin. But if anyone does sin, we have an advocate who pleads our case before the Father. He is Jesus Christ, the one who is truly righteous."

1 John 2:1 (NLT)

According to the Book of Hebrews, Jesus is our High Priest in heaven (Hebrews 4:14). He already atoned for our sins with His death and resurrection. Now, that He has returned to heaven and is with the Father, He acts as **our representative to the Father**, pleading in our behalf.

Have you ever had to go to court, because someone filed charges against you? If you had, then you know that the legal system has a language all its own. That's why you need an attorney to represent you to the judge. Jesus is our defence attorney to God.

Not only has Jesus made the connection between God and us available, but He keeps that connection strong and stable. Christ's representation assures us that the Father won't change His mind when it comes to our salvation.

There is one more thing Jesus is doing for us in heaven. **He is preparing that special place** reserved for us in the New Jerusalem (John 14:1-2). I don't know what that special place is like, but I tend to think that Christ thinks big. I mean, Jesus has had all eternity to think about our special place and He has formed our bodies with amazing complexity and extraordinary precision. How could our place in heaven not be infinitely more glorious?

> *Jesus is our representative to the Father*
> *Jesus is preparing a special place for us.*

Review

1. What Does Jesus Christ Mean?

2. What Makes Jesus Human?

3. What Makes Jesus Divine?

4. What is Jesus doing for us today? (Two things)

Application

1. Let's pretend that Jesus returns tonight to take you back with Him. Try to imagine what the splendor of your place in the New Jerusalem is like.

2. It's important to know that Jesus gave up His place in heaven to come live among us. Yet, now He lives ruling over everything. (Philippians 2:5-9). Can you imagine what Jesus gave up to live among us?

Prayer Time

When you pray, please remember to thank Jesus for coming to the earth so save us. Ask yourself, "How can you have an attitude similar to Christ's?"

Lesson 3: What Is God Like?

God has many characteristics. For one thing, God has all power (Genesis 17:1). There is nothing too hard for God to accomplish. God, also, knows everything (John 21:17). God knows how large the universe is and all the galaxies and stars within it. God knows how many hairs are on your head (Matthew 10:30). He knows how you were born and how you will die. God knows the thoughts within your heart. God is also everywhere. There is nothing He does not see (Hebrews 4:13). He sees everything you do, whether it is good or evil and He sees how others treat you, too.

However, in this lesson, I don't want to focus on God's abilities. I want to focus on God's ways, His character. What is God like? Is God good or evil? Is He loving or cruel?

In this lesson, you will learn to answer the following questions:

1. How do God's ways compare to human ways?
2. What are God's ways (7 characteristics)?

1. How do God's ways compare to human ways?

"My thoughts are nothing like your thoughts," says the LORD.. "And my ways are far beyond anything you could imagine. For just as the heavens are higher than the earth, so my ways are higher than your ways and my thoughts higher than your thoughts."
Isaiah 55:8-9 (NLT)

Many of our natural inclinations are different from God's. In the human world, we usually fixate on one of a few things. Either we fixate on beauty or power or knowledge or money or family. It's not that these things aren't good, but they are less important than God's ways.

God's ways are higher than our ways. God focuses on matters of the heart, on character. It's God's ways that lead us to tell the truth instead of a convenient lie, or to forgive someone we'd rather hold a grudge over. It's God's ways that teach not to steal, even if we are hungry.

However, I believe our ways can become God's ways (1 Corinthians 2:12, 16). As we learn about God and grow in our relationship with Jesus Christ, our ways can change. Christ can help us to let go of the old fixations that used to possess us. He can help us take on God's characteristics, making us more like God. So, let's take a look at some of God's ways.

God's ways are higher than our ways.

---

2. What are God's Ways?

"Yahweh! The LORD! The God of compassion and mercy! I am slow to anger and filled with unfailing love and faithfulness. I lavish unfailing love to a thousand generations. I forgive iniquity, rebellion, and sin. But I do not excuse the guilty."
Exodus 34:6b-7a (NLT)

In this passage, God uses seven characteristics to describe Himself.

1. God is compassionate. God helps those who cannot help themselves. God provided water for Ishmael and Samson, when they were near ready to die of thirst (Genesis 21:14-19; Judges 15:18-19). God provided a savior to rescue the Israelites from the Aramean oppression, at a time when they really didn't deserve it, because He was compassionate (2 Kings 14:23-27). It was Jesus' compassion which caused Him to heal the sick, cast out demons and to teach the crowds (John 5:1-9; Luke 13:16; Mark 5:1-20; Mark 6:34; Matthew 9:35-36).

2. God is merciful. To say, God is merciful or gracious, speaks of more than just forgiveness. It also speaks of God's favor and His generous blessings. If all God did was forgive me of my sins, then that would have been enough for me. But that's not enough from God's point of view. God is not trying to give us just enough. He's trying to give us the very best of what He has. That's why He does more than just save us. He adopts into His family. He gives us an eternal inheritance in His kingdom, and He equips us to overcome the enemy.

3. God is patient. God does get angry, but He doesn't anger easily (2 Peter 3:9, Psalms 103:8; 145:8-9). Think of all the times you sinned before you became a Christian. Aren't you glad that God didn't beat you down every time you lied or swore or stole from somebody? Think about all the people who have cursed God. You don't see God striking them with lightning bolts every time they curse Him, do you?

4. God is loving. Love is sacrificial. It is the giving up of oneself for another (1 John 3:16). God shows His love to us in many ways, but the most obvious way is through His son, Jesus Christ. All of the sins which we committed had to be accounted for. Somebody had to bear the penalty. That's why God gave us His son (John 3:16). Through His death on the cross, Jesus took our sins and the punishment which we deserve, so that we wouldn't have to suffer it (2 Corinthians 5:20-21).

5. God is faithful. The root word for faithfulness is also used for the word "truth" (Strong's Hebrew 529, 571, and 539). To be faithful is to be true. It's to be trustworthy, reliable, a promise keeper. God never lies (Hebrews 6:18). God is like the sun which rises and sets at reliable times. God is like a mirror which reveals exactly how you look—both the good and the bad.

6. God is forgiving. God offers forgiveness to everyone who asks. Just come to God believing and He's ready to forgive. It doesn't matter how many times you sinned against God, or how grievous the sin was (Psalms 103:2-3). God forgives mass murderers just as readily as He forgives cookie jar thieves. When you ask God to forgive you, your sins are dead. God never holds them against you again. (Psalms 103:12)

7. God is just. Just because God is eager to forgive doesn't mean God overlooks people who won't repent. God remembers *everything* they do. Every trifle word you speak—you will answer to God for (Matthew 12:36). Let's face it. God doesn't always judge us in this life. Sometimes the righteous die and the wicked prosper (Isaiah 57:1; Jeremiah 12:1). That doesn't mean they won't be judged. God is eternal—He's got plenty of time.

> *God is compassionate, merciful, patient, loving, faithful, forgiving and just.*

Delayed judgment is not denied judgment. We all have a day when we must stand trial. (Revelation 20:11-15).

Review

1. How do God's ways compare with our ways?

2. What are God's ways (Seven characteristics)?

Application

1. In this lesson I tried hard to dispel many of the myths that people believe about God. Have there been things that you used to believe about God's character that you now understand are false? Please take a moment to write those things down.

2. God is compassionate, merciful, patient, loving, faithful, forgiving, and just. Are there some God-like characteristics that you would like to develop in your own life?

Prayer Time

Please take a moment to pray. Talk to God about how He behaves and ask Him how you can follow in His example. The main thrust of Christianity isn't simply that we learn from Jesus sayings, but that we also learn from actions. We follow His example.

Jesus told His disciples (students) that no student can out-perform his master. The best a student can do is be like his master (Matthew 10:24-25). So, we can't out-perform Jesus. The best that we can become is to be like Jesus. I want you to think about what it means to be like Jesus. Talk to God about developing the character traits which he possesses.

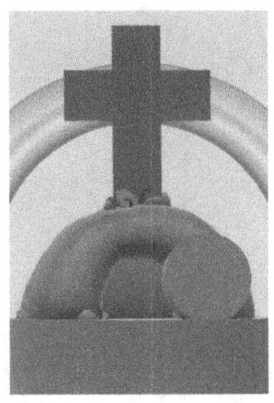

UNIT 3: DEVOTIONS

In the previous lessons we talked about God to try to give you basic understanding of who God is and what He is like, but that's not the same thing as getting to know God personally. When you get to know God personally, you are talking to God and listening to God. You are learning to recognize His voice and understanding what He wants. As you begin to do this daily, you will develop a relationship with God and enjoy shared experiences with Him as He begins the work of transforming your life.

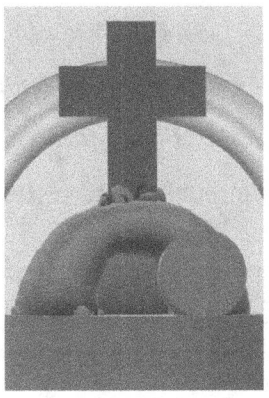

Lesson 1: Prayer

In today's lesson we get to explore prayer. We will discuss how to answer these questions.

1. What is prayer?
2. Why shouldn't you worry about your problems?
3. How should you pray?
4. What should we do if God doesn't answer right away?
5. What should we do when God answers our prayers?

1. What is Prayer?

"Pray like this: Our Father in heaven, may your name be kept holy. May your Kingdom come soon. May your will be done on earth, as it is in heaven. Give us today the food we need, and

forgive us our sins, as we have forgiven those who sin against us.
And don't let us yield to temptation,
but rescue us from the evil one."
Matthew 6:9-13 (NLT)

When we pray, we are making **requests to God.** God answers us in kind. Prayer is the way we talk to a loving Father in Heaven, who wants what is best for us.

In Jesus' time people were abusing prayer (Matthew 6:5-8). Some people would pray out in the street corners really loud for a long time so that other people could see and hear them. These people were pretending to pray to God. Secretly, they were trying to impress others.

Then there was another pretentious group of people who reduced prayer to chanting. They would recite magic words over and over again in a ridiculous attempt to get God's attention.

God does not have trouble hearing you and you should never pray to impress other people. A simple request like, "God, please give me food," carries a lot more weight than a speech like, "OH, GREAT AND MIGHTY AND EXCELLENT EXALTED ONE…" Don't use prayer as a means to manipulate people or God. Just state your request and believe that God will answer you.

Prayer is requests to God.

2. Why shouldn't you worry about your problems?

*Your Father knows exactly what you need
even before you ask him!*
Matthew 6:8b (NLT)

One of the great comforts I experience as a Christian is knowing that when a great problem comes into my life, it did not take God by surprise. God is not up in heaven muttering, "Oh, my, Tim has a problem. What am I going to do?"

God already knows about all our problems. So, if God knows about all my problems, He must also know how He intends to solve my problems. All I need is to ask Him to provide for me the answer He has to my problems.

3. How should I ask God?

"You parents—if your children ask for a loaf of bread, do you give them a stone instead? Or if they ask for a fish, do you give them a snake? Of course not! So if you sinful people know how to give good gifts to your children, how much more will your heavenly Father give good gifts to those who ask him."
Matthew 7:9-11 (NLT)

Probably the biggest hurdle we come against in prayer is **believing that God actually wants to give you good gifts.** A lot of times people think of God as the tyrant in the sky, who is stingy and egotistical and only wants people to grovel before Him so that He can turn them down. God isn't like that at all. God is really a loving Father. He wants us to have good gifts, just like any good father or mother would want their children to have.

God already knows about your problems.

That is why it is so important that we *believe God will answer us* (James 5:1-8). We don't need to sit around wondering, "Oh, my goodness, what if God doesn't…What if…What if…What if…?"

Unbelief negates our prayers. It is like writing the word "VOID" on an already signed check. If half of the time we ask God for things and the other half we worry and complain, what do you think will wind up happening?

Believe that God wants to give you good gifts.

So, don't worry about whether or not God will answer you. God *will* answer you if you trust Him. He might or might not answer you the way you *want* Him to, but He *will* answer your prayer.

4. What if God doesn't answer right away?

"Keep on asking, and you will receive what you ask for. Keep on seeking, and you will find. Keep on knocking, and the door will be opened to you."
Matthew 7:7 (NLT)

Jesus told a story about a poor helpless widow who went to a self-centered judge to ask for justice (Luke 18:1-8). The judge refused to listen to her and sent her away. So, she came back to the judge and asked her for justice again. The judge sent her away again. So, the widow came back to ask the judge again. Every time the judge sent her away, she would keep coming back.

Finally, the judge said to himself, "I'm going to give the widow what she needs, if for no other reason than to get rid of her."

A lot of times people get discouraged when they pray. They ask God for something they need and if God doesn't come through right away, they give up.

Faith is more than simply asking God once and quitting. When we truly believe in something, we don't stop. So, if God doesn't answer us right away, **we need to keep asking.**

God not answering doesn't necessarily mean the answer is, "No." Maybe the answer is, "Not right now," or maybe the answer is, "I have a better idea." We can't always know how God works,

When God doesn't answer right away, keep asking. but we can trust that He has a good reason for what he does. So keep asking.

5. What should I do when God answers my prayer?

Jesus asked, Didn't I heal ten men? Where are the other nine? Has no one returned to give glory to God except this foreigner?
Luke 17:17-18 (NLT)

In Luke 17:11-19, Jesus meets ten lepers along the road. They asked Jesus to heal them, but Jesus didn't heal them. Instead, He told them to go see the priests. In those days, if a person was fully healed of leprosy, he could be accepted back into the community by going to see a priest (Leviticus 14:1-3).

So, they went to the priest, just like Jesus told them. *On the way* to see the priest, their leprosy disappeared. They were now fully healed, but only one of them went back to thank Jesus for the healing.

God loves to give us good gifts. The trouble is many times we don't recognize the good gifts God has *already* given us. We should ask God for things, but we should also **thank God when He answers us.**

Think about the many things you have. Do you have family? Do you have friends? Do you have a home? Do you have food and clothing? Don't take anything you have for granted. Thank God for the good gifts He has given you.

*When God answers your prayers,
Thank God!*

ASK FOR THE IMPOSSIBLE!

"The earnest prayer of a righteous person has great power and produces wonderful results. Elijah was as human as we are, and yet when he prayed earnestly that no rain would fall, none fell for three and a half years! Then, when he prayed again, the sky sent down rain and the earth began to yield its crops."
James 5:16b-18 (NLT)

People often limit God when they pray. They see the need as being so huge and powerful that even God couldn't or wouldn't answer their prayers. Don't be afraid to ask for miracles.

The story James is referring to is the story of Elijah and Ahab (1 Kings 16:29-18:46). King Ahab was terribly wicked and introduced all kinds of idolatry, plummeting the nation of Israel further and further from God. So Elijah told King Ahab, "God says there won't be any more rain until I say otherwise." Then Elijah went off into hiding, because King Ahab wanted to kill him.

Three and a half years later, Elijah challenges the idols' priests to a duel between God and the idols. Of course, God won the duel. So, the Israelites turned back to God. Then Elijah prayed for rain and it rained so hard that it flooded.

What James is saying in these verses is you can pray for the same things as Elijah and trust God to answer your prayers. So, don't be afraid to ask for the impossible, because the impossible might just happen.

I remember one time when I was working, and making barely enough to get by, I knew that winter was coming. I also knew that my expenses would increase and my income would decrease. So, I started looking for a second job. Shortly, after I started looking, the Holy Spirit told me to stop looking for work. He wanted me to focus on my writing instead.

So, I asked God for warm weather, because I knew that if the weather stayed warm, I would not have to worry about paying my bills. Each day I would get up and ask for a warm day. Each day I received it.

After I had done this for a while, the Spirit said to me, "If you ask me, I will give you a warm winter." So, I asked God for a warm winter. For the entire winter, right up until March, I never had to crank up the furnace or suffer a pay cut or pay those huge electric bills. The warm weather was so unusual that it made headlines in the newspaper.

When March came, I did suffer a little cold weather, but not enough to worry me. Spring was right around the corner.

Review

1. What is prayer?

2. Why shouldn't you worry about your problems?

3. How should you pray to God?

4. What should we do if God doesn't answer right away?

5. What should we do when God answers our prayers?

Application

1. When people pray to God about their problems, they generally approach God in one of two ways. Either they focus on the problem and blame God for it. Or, they focus on God and ask Him to resolve the problem. Which type of person are you?

2. The things we are willing to pray for the most are usually the things we want the most. Is there anything you are willing to pray for a long time to receive?

3. When someone does a favor for you, it's appropriate to say, "Thank you." The same is true for God. Try to think of some of the blessings God has done for you, which you can thank Him for.

Prayer Time

Look back at the Matthew 6:9-13, found at the beginning of this lesson. This passage is commonly called *The Lord's Prayer*, because Jesus taught His disciples to pray after this manner. I would like you to pray The Lord's Prayer. While you are praying, think about what The Lord's Prayer means.

When you are done praying, please take time to thank God for any prayer requests He has already answered for you.

Lesson 2: Bible

In today's lesson we will explore the ways that the Bible helps us develop a closer walk with God.

1. Why do we read and meditate on the Bible?
2. Why do we study the Bible?
3. How does memorizing the Bible help us?
4. What happens when we don't obey the Bible?

1. Read and Meditate on the Bible Daily.

Oh, the joys of those who do not follow the advice of the wicked,
or stand around with sinners, or join in with mockers.
But they delight in the law of the LORD,
meditating on it day and night.
Psalms 1:1-2 (NLT)

Where is the best place to find good advice? Can you find it in the newspaper or on television or in a bar or social club? Can you find it in the library or on the Internet or on bulletin boards or painted on the bathroom stalls?

Where do you think the wisest advice comes from? People or God? The best advice comes to us from God. Much of what God thinks about certain topics is already spelled out for us in His word. **God's word was designed to help us live wisely**.

So, it only makes sense that we should *read* and *meditate* on God's word daily. When you read, don't gloss over the words. Think about what you're reading. Understanding the Bible requires depth of thought.

But look at the reward a person receives for having taken the time to read and understand and trust in God's word.

> *"They are like trees planted along the riverbank,*
> *bearing fruit each season.*
> *Their leaves never wither,*
> *and they prosper in all they do."*
> Psalms 1:3 (NLT)

This song goes on to explain that the other path of wickedness leads to destruction (Psalms 1:6). That's where people wind up who wander away from God's word.

Reading God's word is a lot like wearing a seat belt. A seat belt may feel strange, burdensome or even uncomfortable, but in the end, it will save your life. **God's word saves our lives, too.** It saves our lives by steering us away from the sins which would otherwise destroy us (Romans 6:23).

When you read the Bible, you will find it will be helpful to have a plan. Haphazardly picking out random verses is a way many people *misunderstand* the Bible, because they aren't reading the scriptures in context.

Usually, for new believers, the best strategy is to read one book of the Bible at a time, starting with the Gospel of John and Letter of Romans. After spending some time in these books, you may want to go on to read the other Gospels, Paul's Letters and later still, begin reading Acts, the General Letters and Revelation.

Another strategy is to get a Daily Bible or a Daily Bible Reading program to guide you through the entire Bible. Many Bible software packages have programs built right in and some printed Bibles have Bible reading programs at either the beginning or end of the book.

God's word helps us live wisely.
God's word saves our lives, too.

It doesn't matter which plan you use, only that you have a plan that works well for you.

2. Study the Bible

I will study your commandments and reflect on your ways.
I will delight in your decrees and not forget your word.
Psalms 119:15-16 (NLT)

If you read the Bible for a while, you will eventually come across a place (or several places) where you scratch your head wondering, "What does that mean?" Perhaps you've wondered what the Bible says about a specific subject, such as taxes, divorce, love, etc.

This is where the concept of Bible study comes in. Bible studies are designed to help us **understand the Bible more completely** (2 Timothy 2:15).

Most forms of Bible studies involve the use of tools. The tools we use can be as simple as dictionaries or as complex as sophisticated Bible software.

Probably the most essential tools a person could have would be a Bible dictionary and a concordance. These two tools usually don't cost much, but are some of the most useful Bible tools available.

If you want an in-depth study without doing a lot of page turning, a good study Bible or a good Bible software package would probably be better. These study tools usually cost more, but the convenience and quality that they offer are well worth it.

[For more information on Bible study tools, see the back of the book, Resource 2: Bible Tools, IV. Bible Study Tools.]

3. Memorize the Bible.

> *"I have hidden your word in my heart,*
> *that I might not sin against you.*
> *I have recited aloud all the regulations you have given us."*
> Psalms 119:11, 13 (NLT)

The Bible should never be something we merely read like a newspaper. Usually, as soon as we stop reading the Bible, we begin forgetting it. Bible memorization helps us to retain God's word longer and more accurately.

When we hide God's word in our heart, it becomes a part of us. It **keeps us living a righteous life**. Why is that important?

It is important, because our natural bend is to go any other way, but placing God's word in our hearts helps to correct us, to keep us going straight.

Bible study helps us understand the Bible more completely.

> *"The human heart is the most deceitful of all things, and desperately wicked. Who really knows how bad it is?"*
> Jeremiah 17:9 (NLT)

How would you like **to know exactly what God wanted** you to do in a particular situation? Bible memorization brings you closer to that goal. When we accurately quote scripture, we can speak with authority, because we're not speaking our own words, but God's.

As I suggested a plan with Bible reading, I suggest a plan with Bible memorization. As you read, you will probably find any number of verses that stick out in your mind as being important. So, why not memorize them?

It usually works best to work on the same memory verse each day for a week. When the next week comes, work on a new memory verse, but you still need to keep reviewing the old memory verses, so you don't slowly forget them.

Bible memorization takes a lot of patience and it requires more work than merely reading. However, the rewards it offers are well worth it, not only for you, but for other Christians, too.

Bible memorization helps us —
Live right and know God's will.

---

4. Obey the Bible.

"But don't just listen to God's word. You must do what it says. Otherwise, you are only fooling yourselves."
James 1:22 (NLT)

Many people read and read the Bible, but never get anything out of it. Others read the Bible, but only find dread and condemnation. There's a good reason why some people don't profit from reading God's word. They don't understand the Bible, because they don't believe it (2 Corinthians 4:4).

The Bible is a spiritual book. The only way to understand it is through the teaching of the Holy Spirit (2 Corinthians 2:13-14). The Holy Spirit will *only* help you understand it, if you read it believing (Hebrews 11:6). If you really do believe the Bible, you will begin obeying it (James 2:17).

Apostle James compares reading the Bible with no intention of obeying, as a person who sees himself in the mirror, but then walks away, forgetting what he looked like (James 1:22-24).

Can you imagine getting up in the morning, looking in the mirror to see uncombed hair, smudged lipstick, crumbs on your cheek and then go to work without doing anything about it?

That is what reading the Bible without faith and obedience is like. We think we are being good Christians, because we read the Bible. But that goodness is only imaginary. If we don't apply the teachings of the Bible in our life, **we are really deceiving ourselves.** We are only pretending to be good. We must DO what God tells us to actually become good (Matthew 7:21).

A person who refuses to obey God's word is deceiving him or herself.

Review

1. Why do we read and meditate on the Bible? (Two things)

2. Why do we study the Bible?

3. How does memorizing the Bible help us? (Two things)

4. What happens when we don't obey the Bible?

Application

The reason why I designed this book this way, is to get new Christians into the habit of praying and reading the Bible. That's why I've included so many Bible quotations in this book. When you are done reading this book, you will have to develop your own plan for reading, studying or memorizing the Bible.

I'd like you to take a few minutes to think of a plan for the time you spend in the Bible when you are done reading this book. What are you planning to do?

Prayer Time

As you pray today, write a list of some other Christians who you know and pray for them. If you are aware of any specific needs that they have, please bring them up in prayer as well.

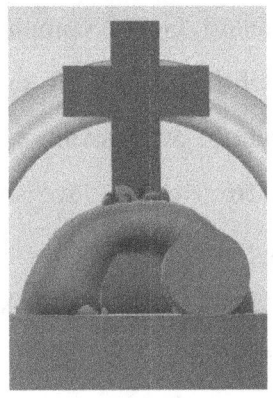

Lesson 3: Praise

Today, we will explore the ways we celebrate God.

1. What does praise do for us?
2. What makes praise a sacrifice?
3. Why should we praise God in hardships?
4. What are you going to do to praise God today?

1. Why should we praise God?

"Go and celebrate with a feast of rich foods and sweet drinks,
and share gifts of food with people who have nothing prepared...
Don't be dejected and sad,
for the joy of the LORD is your strength!"
Nehemiah 8:10 (NLT)

The Israelites had gathered to hear God's words from Ezra and Nehemiah. As they heard God's commandments, they began crying, because many of them had not been obeying God's word. God's word is not meant to bring sadness, but joy into our lives, because it purges sin from us. So, we should be cheerful and rejoice over God's many good works that He has done for us.

Praise strengthens faith. It makes our resistance to temptation stronger. Praise changes our attitudes. It turns the act of serving God from a tedious chore into a delightful reward.

Please don't misunderstand me. I'm talking about praising, not singing. Praise is anything that celebrates God, anything that makes God's greatness shine (Strong's Hebrew 1984). Not everyone can sing well, but everyone can praise God well.

Singing is only one form of praise. There's also dancing, boasting about God's greatness or great works, playing a musical instrument and many other ways to praise God (Psalms 150). If all you do is say, "God is great!" or "God saved me!" then you have at least in some small way begun to praise God.

2. What makes praise a sacrifice?

"Therefore, let us offer through Jesus a continual sacrifice of praise to God, proclaiming our allegiance to his name."
Hebrews 13:15 (NLT)

Praise is a sacrifice, which creates humbleness. When we praise God, we are constantly focusing on God's greatness and marvellous works. So, what are we NOT thinking about?

We are not thinking about ourselves. I don't know how praise works for you, but I can't get caught away in a celebration of God's greatness and worry about my bills at the same time.

When we honor God and lift up His name, we are placing God above ourselves. We are saying,

Praise strengthens our faith

"God is great. God is wonderful. God is amazing." We are NOT thinking, "Oh, look at me. I'm not strong enough. I'm no good," or, just as bad, "Look at me. I can do anything. I'm such a good person."

Praise keeps our focus on God, not on ourselves, which is where it should be.

3. Why should we praise God in trials?

We can rejoice, too, when we run into problems and trials, for we know that they help us develop endurance.
Romans 5:3 (NLT)

Praise makes us humble

Sometimes we go praising God and then we run into a difficult situation. Suddenly all chaos breaks loose, our lives are devastated and God seems far away. How does that make you feel about praising God? It makes you want to quit, doesn't it?

But a Christian who loves God can praise Him in any circumstance. When we experience great hardships, that is the most important time to praise God. **That's when the strength of our faith is *really* being tested.** When a Christian endures hardship, it can only end in one of two ways. Either the Christian will become stronger and closer to God or the Christian will become weaker, more distant towards God.

Having a cheerful attitude and praising God when enduring these hard times helps your faith become stronger. You'll be able to look back at the hardship and say, "Wow. It's amazing that God brought me through all of that."

4. What can I praise God for?

Praise God for saving you from condemnation. Praise God, because He is good to all. Praise God, because He is supreme. Praise God, because He has given you an eternal home in the New Jerusalem. Praise God, because He has forgiven all of your sins. Praise God, because He has given you the Holy

> *When we experience hardships our faith is being tested.*

Spirit. Praise God, because He has given you the Bible. Praise God, because He has given you food to eat and clothes to wear. Praise God, because He has given you a family of Christians. Praise God for loving you. Praise God for making you holy. Praise God, because you can talk to Him any time of any day. Praise God, because He has given you eternal life. Praise God, because He has freed you from being a slave to sin. Praise God because He is always with you. Praise God, because He has all power. Praise God, because He understands you. Praise God, because He is patient with you. Praise God, because He has many riches He desires to share with you. Praise God, because He chose you from the beginning. Praise God for preparing a destiny for you. And, well…you think of a few things to thank God for.

You can praise God for anything!

Review

1. What does praise do for us?

2. What makes praise a sacrifice?

3. Why should we praise God in hardships?

4. What are you going to do to praise God today?

Application

Alright, it's time. Find a way to praise God. You can sing. You can dance. You can clap your hands. You can shout. You can hold up your hands. You can run circles around the room. Get wild or be mild. Just celebrate God.

Act like you're at a party. Act like you're already in heaven. Act as if God is standing right next to you. Act as if there are angels, dancing and singing with you. You can laugh. You can cry tears of joy. Just celebrate the awesome wonder of our God.

UNIT 4: THE CHURCH

Have you ever felt like you were the only Christian out there? I have lots of times. When I was thirteen in New York, there were times when I felt like I was the only Christian in my school. Christ never intended for His students to live in isolation. That is why He founded the Church. Through the Church, we build lasting relationships with other believers, both in this life and in eternity.

Lesson 1: God's Family

Have you ever wondered why church is such an important part of Christianity? It's not enough to simply know God. When we leave our old lifestyles to become a Christian, we develop new lifestyles which include other Christians.

Sometimes it's hard to live as a Christian, because all your old friends are constantly trying to drag you back into sin. The church offers you friendship with other Christians, who can help you stand firm against that temptation.

In today's lesson you will learn how to answer some of the basic questions dealing with the Christian church.

1. What is the family of God?
2. Where did the church come from?
3. Why is church attendance important?

1. What is the Family of God?

For all who are led by the Spirit of God are children of God. So you have not received a spirit that makes you fearful slaves. Instead, you received God's Spirit when he adopted you as his own children. Now we call him, "Abba, Father." For his Spirit joins with our spirit to affirm that we are God's children. And since we are his children, we are his heirs.

Romans 8:14-17a (NLT)

God does not intend Christians to live in isolation. He intends for us to be part of a family. God's family consists of the **Father, the Son, and us.** When we become Christians, we receive the Holy Spirit and the Holy Spirit makes us God's children.

This is completely unlike the way we used to live. When we lived our own sinful ways, we did not have a true spiritual father. We had a taskmaster—our sins turned us into fearful slaves. Anyone who is a slave to sin is afraid of getting caught. Yet, you have to keep doing the sin over and over again, because you are enslaved to it.

But when we gave our lives to Jesus Christ, the Father adopted us into His family and the Holy Spirit came into our lives, filling us with God's love and presence. Notice that we are not part of God's family the same way Jesus is. Jesus is God's Son by birth (John 3:16). We are God's sons and daughters by adoption. This means that we were not always part of God's family. We used to be slaves to sin, instead. God rescued us from sin and adopted us into his family.

What's important to understand is that other Christians are also part of God's family. The Holy Spirit is in them, just like He is in you. That is why when we come together in church services, we call each other brothers and sisters (Galatians 1:2).

Family of God: Father, Jesus, & Us.

Every family has something in common. In a natural family, everyone shares the same genes. In God's family, everyone shares the same Holy Spirit.

2. Where did the Church come from?

You are members of God's family. Together, we are his house, built on the foundation of the apostles and the prophets. And the cornerstone is Christ Jesus himself. We are carefully joined together in him, becoming a holy temple for the Lord.
Ephesians 2:19b-21 (NLT)

In a generic sense, the word church means, any group of people that have come together (Strong's Greek 1577). However, when we are speaking of the Christian church we are talking about a group of Christians who have come together (Matthew 18:18-20).

It is important to know that the church was **Jesus'** idea (Matthew 16:18). Jesus' first church was the twelve apostles. Later, these apostles established other churches (Acts 14:23).

In Ephesians, Paul compares the church to a temple, a house of God. Now, every building has a foundation and the church is no different. As, you know, no building will stand long without a good foundation (Matthew 7:24-27).

For us, the foundation of the church is the **apostles and prophets**. We have their teachings recorded for us in the New Testament. So, as we live following their teachings, we learn to become more like Jesus Christ (Philippians 3:17).

Jesus Christ is the cornerstone—the most vital part. In modern construction, we would say, Jesus is the footing, because in modern construction the footing is the stone which touches the ground. It holds up every other part of the building. If we would compare Jesus to a human body, we would say Jesus is the heart, because the heart is the most vital part of the body. No human can live without a heart.

The ministry and teachings of Jesus Christ were given to us by the apostles (Matthew, Mark, Luke and John). So, as a Christian church, we grow, following the apostles, who are in turn following Jesus Christ (1 Corinthians 11:1).

3. Why is attending Church important?

Let us think of ways to motivate one another to acts of love and good works. And let us not neglect our meeting together, as some

people do, but encourage one another, especially now that the day of his return is drawing near.
Hebrews 10:24-25 (NLT)

A person can be a Christian and not attend church. If you go door to door witnessing, you will find a lot of people who call themselves Christians, but don't attend any type of church at all. Why is that, I wonder? I can't hope to know every reason, but sometimes it's because someone gets offended. Someone becomes mad at someone else in the church.

Founders of the church: Jesus, the Apostles and Prophets.

So, rather than deal with the problem, they run from it. They don't simply move from one bad church to another church. They conclude that all churches are bad and quit.

Another reason why many people quit going to church is because they are distracted by other things. I've met people who couldn't go to church, because that would take time away from their family or from their work.

Also, sometimes people quit church, because a major crisis enters their life and they feel like they must solve the problem all on their own. They don't draw strength from the church to help them or can't find anyone in the church willing to help them.

Many of these un-churched Christians that I have met were selfish. They thought only about themselves or only about their families. They seemed to be spiritually weak, unable to resist temptation and even immature. I remember one un-churched Christian I met who I wondered if he was even Christians at all.

The simple fact of the matter is **Christians draw strength from other Christians** (Proverbs 27:17). We can weather any storm better when we struggle together. We can resist temptation better when we are facing it together. And nobody knows everything there is to know about Jesus. So, we grow as Christians by learning from each other.

Remember that no athlete goes very far without a coach encouraging him, prodding him along. So, no Christian goes very far without support from other Christians.

Christians draw strength from other Christians!

Review

1. What is the family of God? (Three things)

2. Where did the church come from? (Three things)

3. Why is church attendance important?

Application

1. It is important that we be faithful in attending church on a regular basis. Do you have a home church that you can attend, yet? If so, what is the name of the church and what is it like? If not, what church will you most likely be visiting this upcoming weekend?

2. When looking for a home church, the two of the most important things to me are that finding a church which makes frequent reference to the Bible and finding a church where the congregation members genuinely love each other. How can you know whether or not the members of a church congregation love each other?

Prayer Time

As you pray, try to think of any problems you might have concerning your church. If you are in need of finding a home church, you might want to pray for that. You might pray for any special needs the church has or you might want to consider praying for any people you know who have needs in your church.

Lesson 2: Baptism and the Lord's Supper

1. What is water baptism?
2. What does baptism mean?
3. What is the Lords Supper?
4. What is Lords Supper supposed to do for us?

1. What is water baptism?

After his baptism, as Jesus came up out of the water, the heavens were opened and he saw the Spirit of God descending like a dove and settling on him. And a voice from heaven said, "This is my dearly loved Son, who brings me great joy."
Matthew 3:16-17 (NLT)

Water baptism is a person's initiation rite into God's family (the church). Almost any type of society involves some rite of passage for new members. For example, if you want to join a fraternity or sorority at college, you must go through some form of ceremony. If you want to be a voter, you must register to vote. The rite of passage could be as simple as signing a piece of paper or as complex as a week-long ceremony.

For becoming a member of God's family, the initiation is simple. You come to some body of water (a baptistery, pool, river, etc.) There, another Christian will **wash or dip you with water.** Then you leave the water and dry off. This is called baptism.

Jesus was baptized because it was his means of obeying God's commands (Matthew 3:15). Christians should be baptized for the same reason. Jesus even commanded his disciples to baptize new Christians (Matthew 28:19).

Baptism is when a Christian washes or dips you with water to celebrate your new life in Christ.

So, if you are a new Christian, try to be baptized as soon as you have the opportunity. Even if you have been a Christian for years and you haven't been baptized, try to get baptized as soon as you have the opportunity. Don't miss out on the celebration of a new life in Christ.

2. What does water baptism mean?

Well then, should we keep on sinning so that God can show us more and more of his wonderful grace? Of course not! Since we have died to sin, how can we continue to live in it? Or have you forgotten that when we were joined with Christ Jesus in baptism, we joined him in his death? For we died and were buried with Christ by baptism. And just as Christ was raised from the dead by the glorious power of the Father, now we also may live new lives.

Romans 6:1-4 (NLT)

Baptism shows us what takes place when we become saved. Specifically, baptism **represents repentance** (Matthew 3:11). When we repent, we turn from our old sinful lifestyles and turn to God who gives us a new life apart from sin.

Let me give you an illustration. Let's say you live in the country and you are trying to visit a friend who lives in the suburbs just past a big city. On the way to your friend's home, you get lost in the big city and wind up on the wrong highway. What should you do?

What you should do is turn around and get on the right highway. Yet, many people don't do that. They keep living their sinful lifestyles, fully aware that their sins will one day kill them.

God doesn't want us to be like that. God wants us to turn from our sins. He wants us to die to our old

Baptism represents repentance or turning from sin.

sinful lifestyles so that we can live a new life in Christ. For it is possible to live a life apart from sin and Jesus Christ is the way we do that (Philippians 4:13).

Living a new life apart from sin is what we call sanctification or holiness. I will talk more about this new life in the next unit of this book.

3. What is the Lord's Supper?

As they were eating, Jesus took some bread and blessed it. Then he broke it in pieces and gave it to the disciples, saying, "Take this and eat it, for this is my body." And he took a cup of wine and gave thanks to God for it. He gave it to them and said, "Each of you drink from it, for this is my blood, which confirms the covenant between God and his people."
Matthew 26:26-28a (NLT)

Depending upon which church you go to, the Lord's Supper may be called different names—communion, sacraments, mass, etc. I will call it the Lord's Supper, because that is what the Bible calls it (1 Corinthians 11:20).

The Lord's Supper is **a form of worship where we eat bread and wine (or juice) to remember the sacrifice of Jesus Christ's death on the cross.** It's important to know that salvation is not free. It cost Jesus his life. We don't pay anything for salvation, because Jesus paid it for us, but the price Jesus paid was tremendous.

The bread represents Jesus' broken body. Jesus was whipped, beaten and nailed to a cross, where he died (Matthew 26:67, John 19:1-3, 16). The wine represents his blood which came out of His beaten, crucified body.

Christ's crucifixion must have been a gruesome sight. Yet, that is what our sins really are. They are something repulsive and horrible. That is why God required Jesus to die such a horrible death (2 Corinthians 5:21).

> *The Lord's Supper is a form of worship where we use bread and wine (or juice) to remember Christ's death on the cross.*

Even in this solemn act of worship, we share an eager hope. We announce Jesus' death *until He comes back* (1 Corinthians 11:26). Yes, we remember the price of Christ's suffering, but we are also remembering His return from heaven. When Christ returns we will share his joys forevermore.

4. What is the Lords Supper supposed to do for us?

But in the following instructions, I cannot praise you. For it sounds as if more harm than good is done when you meet together. . .When you meet together, you are not really interested

> *in the Lord's Supper. For some of you hurry to eat your own meal without sharing with others.*
> 1 Corinthians 11:17, 20-21 (NLT)

Any form of worship can be abused. For example, Christmas is a Christian holiday. It is the celebration of Christ's birth. Yet, many people abuse this holiday by getting drunk. They take a holiday meant for God and family and they use it satisfy their own selfish desires.

The Corinthian Christians were doing this with the Lord's Supper. God instituted this solemn worship to remind them about Christ and for sharing with each other.

Yet, many of them were using the Lord's supper to eat too much and get drunk. Some Christians never got to share in the Lord's Supper, because others were greedy. Also, they would take part in the Lord's Supper with their hearts still divided against each other.

One of the things the **Lord's Supper was supposed to do was bring Christians together**. The twelve disciples all drank from the same cup and ate from the same bread. So, the Lord's Supper is supposed to remind us that that we are all part of Christ's body and all part of God's family.

Paul wasn't trying to discourage the Corinthians from sharing the Lord's Supper. He wanted them to share it the right way.

When you take part in the Lord's Supper or any form of worship, don't think only in terms of what you get out of it. Think about the Christian sitting next to you, too.

> *The Lord's Supper is meant to bring Christians together.*

MY BAPTISMAL EXPERIENCE

When I was nearly 28, I re-dedicated my life back to the Lord. However, I didn't get baptized until I was 30. This was partly because it took nearly a year for me to find a church home and most of the churches I attended did not baptize people very often. Also, I did not really want to be baptized.

When I re-dedicated my life to Christ, it was the Holy Spirit who led me to salvation in the privacy of my own home. I was so overjoyed just to be saved that I never even thought about baptism. Baptism, on the other hand, is a shared experience. I did not want to admit my sins to a bunch of people.

I began thinking about baptism when I met a man who taught that baptism was necessary for salvation. I disagreed with him and still do, but it was then that I began to realize how I had been neglecting baptism.

So, that summer, during a men's rafting trip, I asked my brother to baptize me in the Nantahala River and he agreed. A couple other Christian brothers shared the moment with me.

The hardest part about getting baptized in a river was having to take off my life jacket. The reason why this bothered me is because I am not a good swimmer and I was afraid of getting seized by the river's current. I also knew there was a waterfall just downstream.

But nothing serious happened. The current did not seize me and it was only a moment after I was submerged that I was pulled back up. (It seemed to be a long moment).

What was important was that I obeyed God. I didn't really get baptized for my own satisfaction. I did it because God asked me to.

Review

1. What is water baptism?

2. What does water baptism mean?

3. What is the Lord's Supper?

4. What is Lord's Supper supposed to do for us?

Application

1. Have you been water baptized, yet? If not, please try to arrange a time when you can be water baptized. If you have, what was your experience like?

2. Some churches share the Lord's Supper in every church service. Others do it only on occasion. Yet, every time we share in the Lord's Supper, we should do it while remembering Christ (1 Corinthians 11:25). Have you shared in the Lord's Supper in church? If you have, what was that experience like?

Prayer Time

As you pray today, please remember Christians in other churches or living in other countries. They may be different from your church, but they are Christians, too. Pray for them, in addition to praying for your local church. If you have not had the chance to be baptized, please pray for God to give you an opportunity.

Lesson 3: Giving and Service

1. Why should Christians give?
2. How should Christians give?
3. Why are some Christians different from others?
4. How should Christians use spiritual gifts?

1. Why should we give?

> *It is more blessed to give than to receive.*
> Acts 20:35b (NLT)

One of the ways we worship God is by giving, sharing the money and things we possess. We give for a variety of good reasons.

One of the reasons we give is because giving is a form of insurance. Giving offers us **protection against tragedy**. Whether we realize it or not, we are all likely to fall on hard times sooner or later. God notices whether or not we are giving. So, if we are too stingy to care about anyone around us, how can we expect others to care about our needs?

Another reason we give is because giving offers us the **opportunity to be a blessing** to other people. God created everything. This means that everything we own really belongs to God. So, when we give to others, it is not really us who are giving. Rather, God is giving to others through us. This, in turn, brings God glory. Giving can even help us tell other people the Good News.

Finally, we give because **giving enriches our lives**. God notices when we give and He is our provider. Everything we own, we own because of God. It was God who gave you your education, job, family, health, opportunities, etc.

Sure you have to work for money, but the only reason you *can* work is because God gave you the means. God could have put you in any body, in any family, in any country of the world.

So, God promises us that when we give, God will give to us. This makes giving an investment. When we give, we believe God will give more back to us.

So, we are, in a sense, going into business with God. Whenever someone goes into business, they are hoping to gain more than they invest. That's the reason people invest in stocks or invest in real estate or even why a farmer plants seeds in the ground.

Many people get discouraged over this, because usually, we cannot see how God gives back to us. You can give and give all your life and still die a poor person. But many of the rewards God gives us are not in this life (Luke 14:12-14). In fact, it's better for us, if most of our rewards are not given to us in this life. That's because the rewards we receive in this life are temporary. The rewards we receive in the New Jerusalem last forever.

Giving protects us from tragedy.
It makes us to be a blessing to others.
It enriches our lives.

2. How should we give?

Remember this—a farmer who plants only a few seeds will get a small crop. But the one who plants generously will get a generous crop. You must each decide in your heart how much to give. And don't give reluctantly or in response to pressure. For God loves a person who gives cheerfully.
2 Corinthians 9:6-7 (NLT)

In the end, only you can decide how much you are going to give, but the Bible tells us to **give in proportion to what we have** (2 Cor. 8:11). In other words, God is not out to kill you in giving. If you don't have much to give, then you shouldn't need to give much. But if you do have a lot, you should give more. That's why I encourage you to give at least 10 percent of what you earn. Ten percent is in proportion to what you earn, because the actual amount of money varies as your income increases or decreases.

Obviously, when it comes to giving, more is better. Giving works the same way that investing works in business. The more money you have invested in stocks or bonds, the more money you are likely to make. The more seeds you plant in the ground, the more fruit you are likely to harvest. You can't plant one tomato seed and expect a bumper crop of tomatoes. If you want a bumper crop, you must plant a lot of seeds.

One final thing I would like to say is please don't give with a sour attitude (2 Corinthians 9:7). When we give, we should focus on the reward, not on the sacrifice. Sometimes giving hurts. If you love God, giving will undoubtedly hurt. But if all we think about is how giving makes our lives harder, we won't be able to see the joyful reward that is in front of us. That's why it is important to have a **cheerful attitude** when it comes to giving.

> *Give in proportion to what you have. Give with a cheerful attitude.*

Think about all the lives that are being touched when you give. Think about how giving is God's way of including you in His ministry. Think about the riches that are waiting for you in the New

Jerusalem, riches which can never be taken away. Think about how God keeps on giving to us over and over again. Think about how giving to others helps make you more like God.

3. Why are some Christians different from others?

In his grace, God has given us different gifts for doing certain things well. So if God has given you the ability to prophesy, speak out with as much faith as God has given you. If your gift is serving others, serve them well. If you are a teacher, teach well. If your gift is to encourage others, be encouraging. If it is giving, give generously. If God has given you leadership ability, take the responsibility seriously. And if you have a gift for showing kindness to others, do it gladly.
Romans 12:6-8 (NLT)

In any given church, there are all different kinds of people. There are old people, adults and children. There are men and women. There can be people with different colored skin, tall people, short people, wide people, and thin people.

Not only do we look different, but we act different, too. We have different personalities and different gifts, too. Also, I'm not altogether certain that these are a complete listing of all of God's spiritual gifts. Why? Because there are many more ministries in a church than what is listed here.

For example, some people are gifted at working with children. The church cannot long survive without some type of children's ministry. Yet, children's ministries are not listed here. So, I try to be open to new possibilities, when it comes to spiritual gifts.

What is important is to know why God gave you a gift and how to use it. When I first came to one church, I really did not want to stay there. I didn't know anybody and couldn't find anything in common with most people in there. I used to think to myself, "Why am I even going to this church? No one here is like me."

Then I realized that was the whole point. No one is like me. No one is supposed to be like me. Maybe I'm not supposed to simply grow from this church. Maybe this church is supposed to grow from me, too.

Paul talked about this relationship between different types of Christians by comparing the church to a human body (1 Corinthians 12:12-26). If you've ever looked at your body, you will notice that some parts are different from others. Your hands don't look like your feet and your feet don't look like your ears. Your eyes look completely different from your skin and your legs are probably much longer than your arms.

Yet, every part of your body works together in perfect unity. Your hands and your feet look different, because they do different things. Your feet are built for strength. They support the entire weight of your body. But your hands are designed for grasping and manipulating objects. You can't do that very well with your feet.

So, Paul was saying, don't exclude yourself, because you are different from everyone else. Don't exclude other people who come along, just because they seem different. **God has a different purpose for each of you.**

4. What should I do with my spiritual gift?

For you have been called to live in freedom, my brothers and sisters. But don't use your freedom to satisfy your sinful nature. Instead, use your freedom to serve one another in love. For the whole law can be summed up in this one command:
"Love your neighbor as yourself."
Galatians 5:13-14 (NLT)

Please keep in mind that, when Paul speaks of service here, he is speaking in a broad sense. Service is anything you do to help another Christian. So, teaching can be a service. Encouraging can be a service. Showing kindness can be a service.

This is why God doesn't make any one of us complete. We are parts of each other. We need each other. We are designed to love each other.

If you have ever gone through any heavy grieving, you know that losing someone you love is a lot like getting an arm or a leg chopped off. It's as if you have to completely re-learn how to live your life without that other person.

> *God has a different purpose for each Christian. So, each Christian is different.*

So, God brings us into a family of other Christians so that we can support each other and love each other. That's why God gives you the gifts you have. **So, you can use your gifts to show God's love to others**.

What good is it to have every spiritual gift out there, if you have no love for other people? (1 Corinthians 13:1-3) What is the purpose in even having spiritual gifts? To use spiritual gifts only to help yourself is very shallow. You will find that it does not satisfy. If you think only of yourself, you will find yourself disgusted and depressed.

But if you reach out to Christians around you, you will find that you do have a great purpose. There are a lot of great things which God wants to accomplish through you and your gifts. Maybe they don't seem great to you, but they could be monumental in the lives of others.

> *God gave you gifts so you could show his love to others.*

Of course, you're not a robot. No one can make you love others. You have to make a choice. Love isn't love, if love isn't given freely.

Review

1. Why should Christians give? (Three things)

2. How should Christians give? (Two things)

3. Why are some Christians different from others?

4. How should Christians use spiritual gifts?

Application

1. What are you going to do to give to God through your local church?

2. Of the gifts in Romans 12:6-8, which ones do you believe you are best at?

3. How can you use the gifts God placed in you to love and serve other Christians?

Prayer Time

As you pray today, pray for the financial and ministry needs of your local church. Does your church have any fundraisers that you can sponsor or volunteer in? Ask God to show you a way you can show His love to other Christians in your local church.

UNIT 5: SANCTIFICATION

When we are born again, Christ enters us and begins a process of maturity. As time passes, the old lifestyle we used to gravitate towards begins to lose its luster (Philippians 3:7-8). More and more, the things which used to rule our lives become subjects to the authority of Jesus Christ (2 Corinthians 10:4-5). The new creation begins to take hold of us (2 Corinthians 5:17). We begin thinking and acting differently (Romans 12:2). We even become disgusted with the things we used to love. That's because we are beginning more and more to think and act like a new creation.

In this unit we will discuss how Christians *mature in Christ*. This act of *maturing in Christ* is called "sanctification" or "holy living." It is how we abandon the old way we used to live to adopt a new life in Jesus Christ.

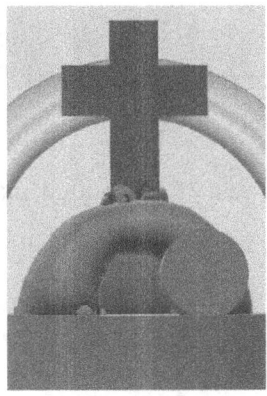

Lesson 1: The Sinful Nature

In this chapter we will learn about some very common wrong ideas people believe about how you are supposed to live after becoming saved.

1. Why can't Christians use God's grace as an excuse to sin?
2. Why can't Christians please God by obeying the law?
3. How does a Christian mature in Jesus Christ?

1. Why can't Christians use God's grace as an excuse to sin?

Do not let sin control the way you live; do not give in to sinful desires. Do not let any part of your body become an instrument of evil to serve sin. Instead, give yourselves completely to God, for you were dead, but now you have new life. So use your whole

body as an instrument to do what is right for the glory of God.
Romans 6:12-13 (NLT)

It's really a very old idea. It's the idea that as long as we keep asking for forgiveness, we can keep on sinning and expect to have a right relationship with God. This type of attitude many people have is rotten.

I don't want to confuse this with another attitude many Christians have where they wonder if God really will forgive all their sins, even though they are having a hard time leaving the sinful life. Yes, God really will forgive you, even if you sinned a hundred billion times.

But that doesn't mean that God's forgiveness gives us an excuse to keep on sinning. Oh, you can find an excuse to keep on sinning, if you want to. You might even find an excuse to sin that sounds good, at first. But the fact of the matter is this, God hates sin and will not let us persist in sinful living.

In Romans 6, Paul gives us some very good reasons why we should stay away from sin. First of all, **we are dead to sin.** (vs.11) That means that our former bondage to sin is annihilated. Jesus died on the cross to save us from our sins. So, Jesus crushed sin's power over us. Sin no longer holds us prisoner. Our sins are now dead and buried.

The second reason Paul gives to stop sinning is **so that we don't become enslaved** to our old sins again. Have you ever tried to eat only one cookie? It's not easy to do. Usually, when you eat one cookie, you get cookies on the brain. Then you can't stop thinking about cookies until you eat another cookie and then another.

Sin is a lot like that. Sin is sticky. Nobody sins only once. When people start sinning they find they cannot stop. If you begin lying, you will keep on lying. If you begin stealing, you will keep on stealing. If you begin getting drunk, you will keep on getting drunk. Jesus said that anyone who sins becomes enslaved to sin (John 8:34).

That's what happens if we go back to sinning after we choose to follow Christ. We go back to that old life of slavery only to find out later on that we can't simply stop sinning whenever we choose.

Lastly, and most importantly, **sin leads to death** (v. 23). If you want to get technical, there is no such thing as a sinful lifestyle. There is only a sinful death-style. You cannot *live* in sin. You can only die from sin. In the same way there is no way to live while drinking poison, there is no way to live while sinning.

You can sin all you want and go back to God asking for forgiveness and expect God to forgive you. But you can't expect God to deliver you from the consequences of all those sins. If you murder someone, you may be

We are dead to sin.
Sin enslaves its victims.
Sin leads to death.

executed. If you drink too much, you might get into a fight and wind up in the hospital or in prison. If you overdose on drugs, you might wind up dead.

All forms of sin ultimately lead to death. Some sins will kill you faster than others. Every form of sinning kills.

Don't be misled—you cannot mock the justice of God. You will always harvest what you plant.
Galatians 6:7 (NLT)

2. Why can't people please God by obeying God's laws?

I love God's law with all my heart. But there is another power within me that is at war with my mind. This power makes me a slave to the sin that is still within me.
Romans 7:22-23 (NLT)

A person can't live life by sinning. If you go back into sin, your sins will destroy you.

However, a lot of people might be wondering, "If I must do good deeds, then why do I even need Jesus Christ? Why not simply obey God's commandments? If I just obey the commandments: don't kill, don't steal, don't commit adultery, then I will be holy and I will be the sort of person God will be pleased with, right?"

Wrong.

Why is this wrong? It is because **without Christ *we are already* slaves to sin**. We have that other power in us that drives us to do evil, even though we really want to do good. That other power is what most people call, the sinful nature.

We inherited this sin nature from Adam, because he was the first human to disobey God. No matter how strong we are, we are not strong enough to defeat the sin nature by ourselves.

When Adam sinned, sin become more than just a one-time act. Sin penetrated every fiber of his being. As such, sin is hard-wired into our bodies. It is embedded in our genetic code. We cannot break our own nature through will power.

Trying to stop sinning through sheer strength is like trying to stop breathing or flapping your arms really hard, hoping to fly. Which do you think is stronger—the Law of Gravity or the human will to fly?

3. How does a Christian mature?

So I say, let the Holy Spirit guide your lives. Then you won't be doing what your sinful nature craves.
Galatians 5:16 (NLT)

When we accepted Jesus Christ, the Holy Spirit saved us from condemnation (Romans 1:1-2). Now, we need to learn how to live under the Holy Spirit's direction, how to follow the Spirit.

Following the Holy Spirit means getting a new attitude (Romans 8:5). We used to think one way, but now we think a different way. We used to live our lives only for ourselves, but now we live for God, instead.

Notice that holy living involves two things. It's not enough to run from the sin. You also have to run toward God. If you try to run from sin, you will find that you are not strong enough or fast enough to escape sin.

Without Christ we are already slaves to sin.

But if you run to God, you will find that all things are possible (Matthew 21:21-22; Luke 1:37). Why is this? It is because the Holy Spirit is stronger than your sinful nature. Let me put it to you this way. Which is stronger—the Law of Gravity, or God, who created gravity? Obviously, God is stronger than gravity.

Holy living is more than just a necessity. It is also a miracle. Only God can take a sinful human being and give him or her a new nature apart from sin. Only God can change your life from something horrible to something wonderful and new.

If you follow the Holy Spirit, He will keep you from sinning.

Review

1. Why can't Christians use God's grace as an excuse to sin? (Three things)

2. Why can't people please God by obeying God's laws?

3. How does a Christian mature?

Application

1. Having the freedom to stop sinning doesn't guarantee that you will stop sinning. Nor does it guarantee that we will be able to quit sinning instantly without a struggle. Which sins would you like God to help you stop doing?

2. Sometimes when we want to stop sinning, an obstacle or another person gets in our way. What obstacles do you have to overcome? What can you do about them?

Prayer Time

As you pray, ask God to forgive you of any sins you may have committed and trust Him for the answer in time. Some Christians stop sinning instantaneously, and for others recovery becomes a struggle, but trust that God will help all the way (Philippians 1:6).

Lesson 2: Following the Holy Spirit

In the last lesson, I briefly talked about the fact that when we give our lives over to Christ, the Holy Spirit sanctifies us by giving us a new mind—a new attitude. We no longer think the way we used to think when we were in sin. Now, I will try to elaborate what I mean by, Follow the Holy Spirit.

1. How do we know if we are following the sinful nature?
2. What are the nine fruit of the Spirit?
3. What is the goal of holiness?

1. How do we know we if we are following the sinful nature?

When you follow the desires of your sinful nature, the results are very clear: sexual immorality, impurity, lustful pleasures,

> *idolatry, sorcery, hostility, quarreling, jealousy, outbursts of anger, selfish ambition, dissension, division, envy, drunkenness, wild parties, and other sins like these. Let me tell you again, as I have before, that anyone living that sort of life will not inherit the Kingdom of God.*
>
> Galatians 5:19-21 (NLT)

The reason why I want to talk about this is because it is important for you to recognize sin in your life. Some sins are obvious. Idolatry, sorcery, and drunkenness are obvious sins. But other sins are less obvious—lustful pleasures, selfish ambition and quarrelling. Anything that is even like this is sinful.

In other words, don't think only in terms of what's on the list. Anything that is similar to these things is sin.

The thing I want you to notice most is that the focus of these attitudes is on self. These are **selfish attitudes** and more than that, these are out-of-control attitudes. These attitudes tend to spiral out of control into worse and worse forms of abuse.

2. What are the nine fruit of the Holy Spirit?

> *But the Spirit produces love, joy, peace, patience, kindness, goodness, faithfulness, humility, and self-control.*
>
> Galatians 5:22-23a (TEV)

Notice how the attitudes of the Holy Spirit differ from the attitudes of the sinful nature. The sinful nature is focused on Me! Me! Me! The attitudes of the Holy Spirit focus more on God and other people.

1. Love - When we love, we give up what we want to meet the needs of someone else (1 John 2:16). Jesus did that by laying down His life to save us from our sins. Now, He expects us to do that for each other (1 John 3:16).

2. Joy - When we are joyful, we are cheerful in any circumstance. This doesn't mean that we will always feel happy. Joy is based on contentment and confidence that God controls what happens to us (1 Timothy 6:8; Romans 8:28).

3. Peace - Peace can mean "to be at rest or to join" (Strong's Greek 1515). When we are at peace with God, we stop sinning and when we are at peace with the people around us, we stop quarrelling with them. In general, a godly person can live in peace, even with his or her enemies (Proverbs 16:7).

4. Patience is what I call, "grace under fire." Patience is what happens when a Christian determines to do good, although faced with hard opposition or circumstances. It is an attitude of—if you curse me, I will bless you. If you steal from me, I will give to you.

If you hate me, I will love you. If you hurt me, I will help you. A patient person does not quit or wear out doing good.

5. Kindness means to help those in need. It also includes forgiving other people. Why did Jesus bother with crowds, healing the sick, feeding the hungry, teaching them about God? It was kindness. Jesus recognized that they were in need and He helped them (Matthew 9:36).

6. Goodness means to have excellent moral character, to lack evil or corruption. Goodness is godliness. It is to be mature in every God-like character trait. Goodness means to resemble God.

7. Faithfulness means to believe, more specifically, to believe God's word (Strong's Greek 4102). Faithfulness is more than just believing one time. It is clinging to the unchanging truth.

8. Humbleness (can also mean gentleness) is to stoop down for others (Strong's Greek 4236; Philippians 2:3). When Jesus became a human, He stooped down to earth. He lived among us and became our servant (Matthew 20:28). Every time Jesus taught the disciples or healed the sick, He was focusing on the needs of those around him. He was serving. You don't see Jesus grasping for wealth or power, because He was too busy helping other people.

9. Self-control is the ability to say "no" to yourself, the ability to deny your cravings. Sometimes we can't have everything we want *right away*. This doesn't mean that God won't supply our needs or even our desires. It only means that sometimes we have wait for the things we desire.

If I see my neighbor has a car I really like, the sensible thing to do would be to save up my money so that I could buy a car like theirs or offer to buy their car. What a person who has no self-control does is try steal, bully or cheat the neighbors out of their car.

Fruit of the Spirit –
Love, Joy, Peace, Patience,
Kindness, Goodness, Faithfulness,
Humbleness, Self-control

---

3. What is the goal of holiness?

For God knew his people in advance, and he chose them to become like his Son, so that his Son would be the firstborn among many brothers and sisters.
Romans 8:29 (NLT)

I have often wondered, what am I striving towards as a Christian? What is spiritual maturity supposed to ultimately be? What will I look like? And the answer is simple. **We become like Jesus Christ.**

Please don't read this statement too literally. We don't have to dress up in a robe and sandals, grow a long beard and say, "Verily, verily." However, if Jesus wore your clothes, went to your job, lived in your house, and lived in your skin, what would He do? If Jesus were you, how would He treat your spouse or your kids or your teachers or your boss?

The very name, Christian means "disciple of Christ" (Acts 11:26). We are students (disciples) of Jesus Christ. We are His followers. So, it only makes sense that we will become like Him.

When we were saved, God automatically made us righteous (Romans 5:1). We were made holy, simply by trusting in Jesus Christ to save us. But now that we are saved, we are learning to walk in that salvation. We are learning to become sanctified, to live the righteous life that was automatically given to us by Jesus Christ.

I have often wondered, well, why does God want me to be like Jesus Christ? What is the point of going through all this work and suffering?

We suffer with Christ so that we can rule with Jesus Christ (Revelation 22:5; 2 Timothy 2:12). Jesus is looking for a few good men and women to govern His kingdom alongside Him. But in order for you to rule with Him, you have to be good.

In the same way that it wouldn't make sense to hire a thief to work as a banker, it wouldn't make sense for God to hand over the rule of His kingdom to an immoral selfish person. If you want to be entrusted with something important, you must prove to be trustworthy.

I don't know exactly what Jesus intends for us to be ruling in His kingdom, although I do know we will be ruling over angels (1 Corinthians 6:1-3). We will rule over angels and ultimately the whole world. But what we will be ruling, specifically, I don't know. What I do know is that God is very creative. Who can imagine what surprises God has in store for us?

Whatever it is that is waiting for us in the eternity, we have a lot to look forward to. That is why it is important to keep moving forward as we become more like Jesus Christ, less like the sinful ways we used to live. As we become more like Jesus, we begin showing His love to the world.

Review

1. How do we identify the sinful nature?

2. What are the nine fruit of the Spirit?

3. What is the goal of holiness?

Application

1. Based upon what you've read in the Bible so far, what does holiness mean to you?

2. Often one fruit of the Spirit leads to another. People who are joyful also tend to be more loving and more patient with other people. Which fruit do you believe God would like to help you develop in your life first?

Prayer Time

As you come to God in prayer today, I want you to focus on the "Do" commands, not the "Don'ts." Focus mostly on having a closer walk with Him and becoming more and more like Jesus Christ. Sanctification is a scary thought for many Christians, because it seems as if we are grasping for the impossible. And we are grasping for the impossible.

Sanctification is a miracle, just like getting saved was a miracle. You couldn't have gotten saved without God's help and you can't get sanctified without God's help, either. So, just trust God to help you accomplish those impossible changes in your life.

Lesson 3: Personal Convictions

1. How do we live among Christians with different personal convictions than us?
2. What do I do if I have a sensitive conscience?
3. What do I do if I have a relaxed conscience?

1. What are personal convictions?

Accept other believers who are weak in faith, and don't argue with them about what they think is right or wrong. For instance, one person believes it's all right to eat anything. But another believer with a sensitive conscience will eat only vegetables.
Romans 14:1-2 (NLT)

When it comes to matters of right and wrong, some things are definitely wrong. For example, is it wrong to steal or cheat someone? Yes, it is definitely wrong (Mark 10:19). However, other matters are more vague. These vague convictions that are not clearly spelled out in the Bible are called personal convictions.

In this scripture, Paul refers to eating meat. Should Christians be allowed to eat meat or should they be vegetarians? There are Christians out there who are vegetarians. They believe that eating meat is wrong and should be avoided entirely. But many Christians believe that there is nothing wrong with eating meat.

It is important to understand that the matter about eating meat is only an example. We could talk about other topics that are not clearly spelled out in the Bible. For instance, should Christians be allowed to drink alcohol? Some churches say, "Yes." Others say, "No." I won't talk anymore about alcohol simply because it is a divisive topic.

Paul is using meat to explain a concept. Some Christians have more sensitive consciences than others. So some actions might be sin for one Christian, but not sin for another. God doesn't always tell each of us the same thing. We are different creatures, after all.

A personal conviction is one that is not clearly spelled out in the Bible.

So, what should we do if someone else believes differently than us? **We should accept them as fellow Christians**. We shouldn't argue about who's right and who's wrong.

2. What if I have a sensitive conscience?

Yes, each of us will give a personal account to God. So let's stop condemning each other…I know and am convinced on the authority of the Lord Jesus that no food, in and of itself, is wrong to eat. But if someone believes it is wrong, then for that person it is wrong.

Romans 14:12-14 (NLT)

Let's pretend that I'm the vegetarian Christian. I believe that eating any form of meat is wrong. But I'm eating dinner with another Christian and I see that Christian take a big bite out of a burger right beside me. What should I do?

If someone has a different personal conviction than you, You should accept them.

Do not condemn a Christian brother or sister for having a more relaxed conscience than you. If he or she believes eating meat is alright, that's none of my business. If that Christian really is sinning by eating meat, that is between them and God.

But if I go around condemning other Christians for doing something that makes me feel guilty, I should be careful that God won't hold that against me on the Judgment Day (Matthew 7:1).

Now, let me ask another question. If I believe eating meat is wrong and I see another Christian eating meat, does that give me permission to eat meat, too? Why?

No. I may not eat the meat. Personal convictions are still a matter of right and wrong. Only, they are a matter of conscience. So, we are not talking about what is right or wrong for everybody. We are talking about what is right or wrong for me.

Don't bend the convictions God placed in your heart for anybody, Christian or not. This is important because bending your convictions often leads to compromise and eventually sin. If God told you something was wrong or if you have doubts about whether or not something is wrong, then it is wrong (Romans 14:23). It doesn't matter what everyone else is doing.

3. What if I have a relaxed conscience?

We who are strong must be considerate of those who are sensitive about things like this. We must not just please ourselves.
Romans 15:1 (NLT)

In this verse the strong are those people who have a strong or relaxed conscience about eating meat. They don't believe eating meat is wrong.

Don't condemn other Christians with more relaxed consciences.
Don't bend your personal convictions.

Let's pretend I am a meat-eating Christian. I believe eating any type of food is good and I don't mind eating meat any time I want. Then I meet up with this vegetarian Christian who is always bothered at the sight of meat. How should I treat her?

I should not let the vegetarian Christian's convictions irritate me. In other words, I **shouldn't get mad or hate** the other Christian for feeling upset around me, if I'm eating meat.

If eating meat is going to upset my vegetarian brother or sister, then I should love my fellow Christian more than I love to eat meat. I should stop eating meat around them.

For some Christians, this can be a serious issue. If a new Christian feels guilty about eating meat, but sees me eating meat, what is that new Christian likely to do? The new Christian will probably start eating meat, too. Even though that new Christian will be sinning, he or she will follow my example.

It's not enough to just follow your own personal convictions. You should always **consider the personal convictions of other Christians**, too. Don't let something that is good for you lead someone else into sin.

The whole point of this lesson about personal convictions is to encourage peace and unity among Christians. I don't believe it would be right for the vegetarian Christians and the meat-eating Christians to separate into two churches: meat-lovers and veggie-lovers.

In the same way, I don't believe it would be right for me to separate from a church for having a few teachings that I don't agree with (1 Corinthians 11:18). So, as Christians, let's not argue over who's right or wrong. Let us simply affirm our love for each other.

Don't hate Christians with sensitive consciences.
Don't tempt Christians to go against their consciences.

Review

1. How do we live among Christians with different personal convictions than us?

2. What do I do if I have a sensitive conscience? (Two things)

3. What do I do if I have a relaxed conscience? (Two things)

Application

1. It's important to know what your personal convictions are. Many times, people don't know what their personal convictions are until they are in a situation which makes them feel guilty. Think of some situations which might make you feel guilty. What would they be?

2. What should you do if you see another Christian do something that you are not sure is right or wrong?

Prayer Time

As you pray, ask God to help you discover the convictions He has placed in your heart. Ask Him to help you be patient towards other Christians who might be sensitive to issues which do not bother you. Also, pray, especially for any Christians who might be irritating you right now.

UNIT 6: SPIRITUAL WARFARE

As Christians, it is important to understand that we have an enemy. There is someone who doesn't want Christians to succeed in living out their faith. He will resist us all the way. Chances are, you've experienced some of this resistance already.

In this unit, we will cover the origin of our enemy, some of the methods he uses to stop or weaken Christians, and some of the ways we can overcome him.

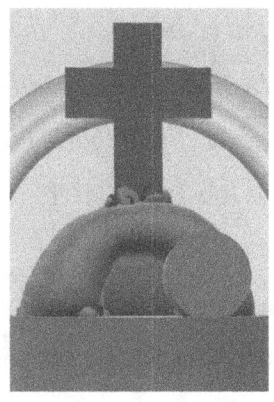

Lesson 1: The Enemy

The focus of the Bible is always on God and Jesus Christ. The Bible says little about our enemy. However, the things the Bible does say about our enemy are very important. That's why Christians should always remain focused on God, but watchful for the enemy. Don't focus on the enemy, but be aware of his tactics and schemes.

1. Who is our enemy?
2. What are demons?
3. What is Satan's destiny?
4. How should Christians react to Satan?

1. Who is our enemy?

One day the members of the heavenly court came to present themselves before the LORD, and the Accuser, Satan, came with

> them. "Where have you come from?" the LORD asked Satan. Satan answered the LORD, "I have been patrolling the earth, watching everything that's going on."
>
> Job 1:6-7 (NLT)

The name of **our enemy is called Satan, or the devil** (Revelation 12:9). His name means "accuser," because his role is a prosecuting attorney in God's court (Strong's Hebrew 7854). Whether people know it or not, we are always being evaluated by God (Psalms 14:2). In God's heavenly courtroom, we are either being condemned or justified.

Now, the devil is a type of evil angel (Ezekiel 28:14-15; Luke 10:18-20). His role is that of an accuser. He goes to heaven in an attempt to get God to condemn us (Revelation 12:10).

He is also called, the "tempter," because he tries to get people to sin (Matthew 4:1, 3). The devil tempted Adam and Eve to sin (Genesis 3:13, Revelation 12:9). He also tempted Jesus Christ to sin (Matthew 4:1-3). Why would the devil try to get people to sin?

If the devil can persuade people to sin, he can get God to condemn us (Romans 5:18). If God condemns people, we will one day wind up in the Lake of Fire forever (Matthew 25:41).

The name of our enemy is Satan or the devil

Ultimately, the devil's goal is to destroy people (John 10:10). Apparently, he can't destroy us by simply killing us. So, he tries to destroy us by persuading us to sin.

The devil is also called, "the ruler of demons" (Mark 3:22-23).

2. What are demons?

Then he [Jesus] will say to those on his left, "Depart from me, you cursed, into the eternal fire prepared for the devil and his angels."
Matthew 25:41 (ESV)

Satan isn't alone in his attempts to overthrow us. He has an army of *angels*, the same way God does (Matthew 25:41; 26:53). Satan's angels are often called demons or evil spirits (Luke 8:2). Essentially, demons are evil angels. Demons are what happens when someone who is as powerful as an angel, becomes thoroughly corrupted.

So, what we know about angels generally applies to demons as well. First of all, **angels and demons are spirit beings** (Hebrews 1:13-14). As such, they have incredibly long life. For example, the same Satan who tempted Job, also tempted Jesus Christ thousands of years later (Matthew 4:10-11). The same Gabriel who gave visions to the Prophet Daniel announced the coming of Jesus Christ to Mary hundreds of years later (Daniel 9:21; Luke 1:26-27).

Angels and demons are powerful. Two angels caused several men in the City of Sodom to come down with blindness (Genesis 19:10). One angel killed the majority of an entire army (2 Kings 19:35). Satan even had the power to cause fire to fall from heaven (Job 1:16).

Angels and demons are organized in ranks, much like an army. In Daniel 10, Daniel fasted and prayed for the Israelites. God sent an angel to speak with Daniel, but the angel didn't arrive for three weeks. The Ruler (Prince) of Persia had been fighting the angel.

Who is this Prince of Persia? The Prince of Persia was a high ranking demon, a type of demon army general. This angel who talked to Daniel would have to go right back to fighting the Prince of Persia.

So, what we actually know about angels and demons is just the tip of the iceberg. There's a lot of invisible warfare that goes on which we humans know nothing about. Demons are most commonly associated with demon possession, but they are also associated with idol worship, some sicknesses and even deception (Luke 8:26-37; 1 Corinthians 10:20; Matthew 9:32-33; 1 John 4:5-6).

Demons are evil spirit beings

3. What is Satan's destiny?

Then the devil, who had deceived them, was thrown into the fiery lake of burning sulfur, joining the beast and the false prophet. There they will be tormented day and night forever and ever.
Revelation 20:10 (NLT)

Satan is the angel who rebelled against God (Ezekiel 28:14-18; Isaiah 14:12-17). He was evicted from heaven, although he still has influence there (Luke 10:18). So, what is Satan's destiny?

The devil is stronger, faster, and smarter than any of us. He's been around a long time and he knows what he's doing. But he is not stronger, faster, or smarter than God.

In the story of Job, every time the devil tried to test Job, God set a limitation on the devil.

- *You can take all Job has, but you can't harm him* (Job 1:12).
- *You can make Job sick, but you can't kill him* (Job 2:5-6).

God controls what the devil is capable of doing.

As such, our enemy has incredibly long life, but not eternal life. **He will be tormented forever in the Lake of Fire**, which is called the Second Death (Revelation 20:14). Keep in mind that the devil is a spirit being. As such, death for him is not a decaying body, but an eternal tormenting of the spirit (Daniel 12:2).

We Christians, on the other hand, have the promise of Eternal Life. You get to live forever, but not Satan. Satan may be stronger, faster, and smarter than you, but you will outlast him.

Satan is <u>not</u> *going to be* judged either. Satan *has been* judged and condemned (John 16:11). Satan is kind of like a prisoner on death row. Only, he's more like a prisoner on death row who wears an ankle bracelet.

Satan has influence. He can go anywhere he wants and do many of the things he wants. But he can't go anywhere out of God's sight and he can't do anything God forbids. So, he's still within God's invisible prison. With everything Satan is doing on the earth, he's only biding his time, awaiting the inevitable.

Satan will be tormented in the Lake of Fire forever!

In a real sense, Satan is as good as dead. Eternal life has already been lost to him. He has no chance of ever recovering it, but he can try to keep you from getting it.

4. How should Christians react to Satan?

Stay alert! Watch out for your great enemy, the devil. He prowls around like a roaring lion, looking for someone to devour. Stand firm against him, and be strong in your faith.

1 Peter 5:8-9 (NLT)

In 1 Corinthians 6, the Apostle Paul told the Corinthian believers to remove an immoral church member from their fellowship. Eventually, this wayward member repented of his sins, but some of the Corinthian Christians wondered if repentance was enough. So in 2 Corinthians 2, Paul told the Corinthians to forgive him.

What reason did Paul give the Corinthians for forgiving this repentant church member? We are aware of the Satan's tricks (2 Corinthians 2:11). As Christians, we should be aware of the tricks Satan uses to throw us off our course.

Satan loves to deal in extremes. If he can't make you unjust, then he will try to make you unforgiving. If he can't make you immoral, then he will try to make you self-righteous.

As Christians, we should **be aware of what Satan's schemes are**. That is why, in the next lesson, I will deal with the most common tactics Satan uses against Christians.

The Apostle Peter also warned us to **watch out for Satan and fight Satan.** As you know, the army never sleeps. Anytime day or night there are always at least a few soldiers standing guard, because the enemy can attack any time. Christians need to be watchful for the enemy, too.

Any moment of the day, from the time you open your eyes in the morning until the time you close them at night is fair game for the enemy.

1. Be aware of Satan's schemes.
2. Watch out for and fight Satan.

You may be tempted. You should expect a temptation. In fact, the time when your enemy most wants to tempt you is the time you least expect it. So, be ready to fight any time.

Review

1. Who is our enemy?

2. What are demons?

3. What is Satan's destiny?

4. How can a Christian prepare against Satan? (Three things)

Application

1. The Bible tells us that our enemy is a spirit. How is that different from the people we tend to consider enemies?

2. The devil's destination is the Lake of Fire, but that doesn't stop him from trying to get us to go with him. Have you ever met someone who had already lost something or was already going to be punished, but tried to drag you down to his or her level?

Prayer Time

I know that we've talked a lot about the enemy today, but I want you to keep in mind that the enemy isn't the only one at work. The devil is working, but God is working, too. God's work will trump the devil's work.

So, as you pray, remember that you are the victor. In many ways you have already triumphed over the devil, because you no longer belong to him. So, thank God for the victory you already have and ask him to protect you from the devil's future schemes.

Pray for people in your church. Ask God to save them from temptation, too.

Lesson 2: The Devil's Schemes

1. What are trials?
2. What do hardships do for Christians?
3. Why do people persecute Christians?
4. How does the devil introduce deception in the church?

1. What are trials?

Count it all joy, my brothers, when you meet trials of various kinds, for you know that the testing of your faith produces steadfastness.
James 1:2-3 (ESV)

If you have ever gone to school, you know that teachers do more than just teach. They also give students tests. Most students fear tests for a good reason. The test reveals how much the student has learned. So, if the student has been lazy about studying, the teacher will know it.

The trials we face in life are just like taking a test. Only, instead of revealing how much we know, a trial reveals our character. A trial is designed to show us what we are really like on the inside.

> *Temptation comes from our own desires, which entice us and drag us away. These desires give birth to sinful actions. And when sin is allowed to grow, it gives birth to death.*
> James 1:14-15 (NLT)

Temptations are always associated with trials. When your character is tried, you will always be tempted to give up on Christ. So, in essence, **a trial is anything that tests our faithfulness to God.** Whenever you are tempted, you are always on trial. In fact, the words for temptation and trials are related and can be translated either way (Strong's Greek 3985, 3986).

In the same way that you cannot have a test without test questions, you cannot have a trial without temptations. Temptations are designed to force you to make a choice. You either choose to do good or you choose to do evil. Either you resist the temptation or you give in to it.

A trial is anything that tests our faithfulness to God.

2. How do we deal with hardships?

We can rejoice, too, when we run into problems and trials, for we know that they help us develop endurance. And endurance develops strength of character, and character strengthens our confident hope of salvation. And this hope will not lead to disappointment. For we know how dearly God loves us, because he has given us the Holy Spirit to fill our hearts with his love.
Romans 5:3-5 (NLT)

One of the tactics the enemy uses to try to get us to stop trusting in God is to grind us down with a very severe hardship. You lose your job. You are evicted from your home. Your husband or wife divorces you. Your children are taken away. Your best friend has just died.

Then when we reach our moment of desperation, we begin to face our real self. Do we really believe in Jesus, even though it means losing loved ones, money, possessions, etc.?

When we endure hardships, one of two outcomes will happen. Either our faith in God weakens or it gets stronger. It never stays the same.

What determines whether your faith is stronger or weaker? You do. It's **the attitude** you carry into the trial. Either you will begin to complain and doubt God or you will cling to God and trust him more.

The more hardships you have to endure, the stronger your faith becomes. It's just like lifting weights. In order for your faith to become strong, you must endure resistance. The heavier the weight, the stronger your muscles become. The fiercer the hardship, the stronger your faith becomes.

So, even though the devil uses hardships to destroy our faith, God uses them to strengthen our faith. In this way, the devil simply becomes another tool **God uses to bring us closer to himself**.

3. Why do Christians suffer persecution?

God blesses you when people mock you and persecute you and lie about you and say all sorts of evil things against you because you are my followers. Be happy about it! Be very glad! For a great reward awaits you in heaven.
Matthew 5:11-12a (NLT)

See if this experience sounds familiar? You have just given your life to Jesus Christ. All of your sins are forgiven. You are on your way to heaven. God is on your side. You feel as if you are walking on clouds. All of that old life is gone—good riddance. Now, you have a wonderful new life with

> *If we have the right attitude, God will use trials to bring us closer to himself.*

Jesus Christ. Everything is going wonderful…until you get home.

Then all of a sudden, people think you're strange or weird. Your old friends at work or school begin to shun you. They act as if they don't know you or they hate you or they fear you like some terrible disease.

If you have experienced anything like this, then you probably know what I'm talking about. It's called persecution. It's when people treat you in a hateful manner for being a Christian or for doing good.

Persecution can come from anybody who knows you, but it hurts the most when it comes from close friends and family members (Matthew 10:34-39). Why do people hate those of us who become Christians?

It is because *we are no longer one of them* (John 15:18-19). We can't get drunk with them. We can't abuse others with them. We can't lie to cover up their sins. There are a lot of things that they can do which we, Christians, cannot.

Christianity offends evil people, because it exposes their sins. When Christians stop living evil lives and begin living clean godly lives, it makes unbelievers feel guilty, even envious.

It's like being a B student in school, while having an A student for a brother. If your brother or sister is constantly out-performing you, you're going to be tempted to act a little envious.

Christianity offends evil people, because it exposes their sins.

Even if you're doing a good job, you're still going to feel inadequate, because you're not going to be as good as your brother.

That is what it's like for unbelievers who live around dedicated Christians. Suddenly, they feel inadequate, as if their evil deeds were exposed by a bright light (Matthew 5:14). Rather, than repent of their sins, many of them take it out on you. They can't ascend to your level of goodness. So they try to drag you back down to their level. They try to make you become like them.

Understand that it's not you that they hate—it's the light. It's actually the Spirit of Jesus Christ (Holy Spirit) who lives inside of you. So, when they harass you, it is not because they hate you. It is because you represent Jesus Christ (John 8:12; 1:1-5). They are persecuting Christ, just as they did 2000 years ago.

You should also understand that being persecuted is a way of knowing that you are a true believer. Every godly person gets persecuted (2 Timothy 3:12). Every person who really loves God, gets hated by the world. So, if following Jesus causes other people to hate you, what does that tell you about your relationship with God?

But I say, love your enemies! Pray for those who persecute you! In that way, you will be acting as true children of your Father in heaven. For he gives his sunlight to both the evil and the good, and he sends rain on the just and the unjust alike.

Matthew 5:44-45 (NLT)

4. How does Satan deceive Christians?

These people are false apostles. They are deceitful workers who disguise themselves as apostles of Christ. But I am not surprised! Even Satan disguises himself as an angel of light. So it is no wonder that his servants also disguise themselves as servants of righteousness.
2 Corinthians 11:13-15 (NLT)

Another trick the devil uses to drive Christians back into sin is deception. Lies are about as old as the devil himself (John 8:44). It was lying which caused Eve to eat the forbidden fruit (2 Corinthians 11:3).

Usually the way the devil deceives Christians, is through sinful messengers. Sometimes these sinful people disguise themselves as other Christians and sometimes they don't. This person will have a message that sounds good, but often contradicts the teachings of scripture.

The way you tell whether or not a messenger is from the devil is by examining his or her lifestyle (Matthew 7:15-20). Crooked messages come from crooked people. If this person is lying, stealing, greedy, committing sexual immorality or engaged in other vices, then you know this person is not from God (Jude 1:11).

Don't be fooled by the *title* a person has, either. Many times people will try to use their titles as a smokescreen to promote their immoral ideas. They might say, "I know what I'm talking about, because I'm an expert."

I'm not going to suggest that we should abandon science or philosophy or any other field of study. But I will suggest that if you hear a message from an "expert" which sounds immoral or ungodly, you should get a second opinion.

One thing I've learned about experts, in any field of study, is that they often are in disagreement with other experts. This is especially true when it comes to morals. Can you imagine why?

> *The devil often deceives Christians through sinful messengers.*

Experts are tested on what they know, not on their moral character. So, there can be any number of good experts or evil experts out there.

Experts who use their titles to promote immorality are trying to distract you. It's an old magician's trick. "Look at my right hand. Don't pay any attention to what my left hand is doing."

Also, don't be fooled by the titles reverend or pastor or priest, either. The devil has his clergymen, too. You can tell whether they are from God or from the devil by whether they are living a godly or immoral lifestyle (Matthew 7:15-20).

Now, don't go spying your pastor, but if you notice the minister in your church is sinning repeatedly, you should stay away from him or her. Why? Because he probably already has a very detailed excuse for his sin. If you confront him, he will only try to make you feel guilty and confused. He might even try to get you to sin, too (2 John 1:10, 11).

Also, try not to not get discouraged by wicked clergyman. God will eventually judge them for all the lies they have spoken and for all the people they have led astray (Matthew 18:6; Galatians 1:9; 2 Peter 2:1-3).

In the end, there is only one cure for deception. It is the truth. That is why I always compare any new messages I read or hear with what I read in the Bible (John 8:31-32).

Review

1. What are trials?

2. What do hardships do for Christians?

3. Why are Christians persecuted?

4. How does Satan introduce deception to the church?

Application

1. What kinds of trials, temptations, or persecutions are you dealing with right now?

2. In what ways can you show God that you trust Him, despite the trial?

3. Is there anyone you know who is giving you a hard time that you can pray for?

Prayer Time

As you pray, take time to remember that, for every temptation you face, there will also be a reward to enjoy in heaven. So, ask God to help you with the trial, but also thank Him for the deliverance and thank Him for the reward you will receive. Also, pray for those who hate and persecute you that God would help them turn away from sin. Generally, the people who hate Jesus the most are the ones who need Jesus the most.

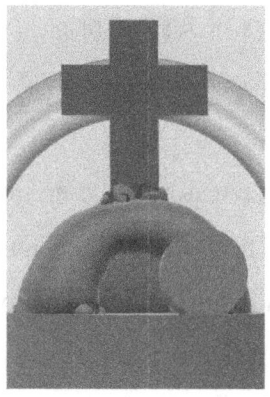

Lesson 3: God's Mighty Champions!

(Inspired by Judges 6:12)

In today's lesson we will learn some of the ways that we can defeat the devil.

1. Why does God call Christians champions?
2. How do hardships affect our victory?
3. What types of weapons do Christians fight with?
4. How did Jesus overcome?

1. Why does God call us champions?

For every child of God defeats this evil world, and we achieve this victory through our faith. And who can win this battle against the world? Only those who believe that Jesus is the Son of God.
1 John 5:4-5 (NLT)

Every person who trusts in Jesus Christ is God's Champion. You might not look or feel like a champion, but that doesn't change the fact that you are one.

Probably the greatest honor that God can give any one of us is to be called, "A Child of God," because that means the King of the Universe has adopted you into His loving family and given you an eternal inheritance.

But the second greatest honor must be when God calls us His Champions. When God calls us Champions, He is saying that we have defeated all of the trickery of the devil. We resisted him and we defeated him. That's why God calls us His Champions.

What is it that makes us God's Champions? It is **our faith,** our total reliance on God to take care of us through every temptation of the enemy.

Do you remember what happened when you got saved? That little bit of faith that you used to call upon God pulled you out of Satan's clutches. You are no longer his slave, no longer blinded by devils lies. Choosing Christ was the single most critical battle in your life—and you won it!

Now, we are in Christ and Christ is defeating the devil. So, we are defeating the devil, too! (1 Corinthians 1:30; 2 Corinthians 2:14) As Christians, we will receive an eternal inheritance. So, the most important thing for us to do is to hold onto that

God calls us his Champions because we are defeating the world by our faith.

victory. For us, the most critical battle has already been won, even though there are still many battles left to win.

2. How do hardships affect our victory?

Can anything ever separate us from Christ's love? Does it mean he no longer loves us if we have trouble or calamity, or are persecuted, or hungry, or destitute, or in danger, or threatened with death? . . . No, despite all these things, overwhelming victory is ours through Christ, who loved us.
Romans 8:35, 37 (NLT)

A lot of times Christians get discouraged. They believe that if God allows tragedy, destitution, severe hardships or handicaps to happen to them, that must mean that God has abandoned them. Nothing could be further from the truth.

Every mother knows that when she sends her kids off to school, that kid of hers is going to face hardship at that school. Someone's going to call her boy names or pull his hair or step on his toes. If the mother keeps on sending her son back to school, does it mean she does not love him?

Perhaps one reason God allows Christians to struggle is because He believes we can overcome them (1 Corinthians 10:13; Revelation 3:21) Yes, God is bold enough to believe that we can crush the devil, even if we are fighting with a handicap (2 Corinthians 12:7-10).

If God is faithful to believe in us, what stops us from believing in God? **Our struggles only affirm that we are mighty champions.** After all, how can a person claim victory without being tested? How can a person become a champion without resistance?

God's plan for our lives is to defeat the devil through us, making us His mighty champions.

> *The God of peace will soon crush Satan under your feet.*
> Romans 16:20 (NLT)

3. What types of weapons do Christians fight with?

We are human, but we don't wage war as humans do. We use God's mighty weapons, not worldly weapons, to knock down the strongholds of human reasoning and to destroy false arguments. We destroy every proud obstacle that keeps people from knowing God.
2 Corinthians 10:3-5a (NLT)

So, the next question is, "How will we defeat the devil?"

Christians do *not* make war the same way that most people make war—with tangible weapons—guns, bombs, and missiles.

Christian weapons are *not* tangible; you can't buy them in the store. Our weapons are **spiritual weapons—weapons of the heart**. We convert people; we *don't* destroy them. That is because we know that our real enemy is the devil, not people (Ephesians 6:12).

Our weapons are powerful. They can tear down demonic strongholds. A stronghold is like a castle (Strong's Greek 3794). It's an enemy fortification that cannot be easily captured. These are the castles we tear down: corrupt human reasoning, proud obstacles, and evil thoughts (vs.5).

Our struggles affirm that we are God's Champions!

Our warfare isn't against people—it's really against the devil's lies and temptations. All of us were originally deceived (Revelation 12:9). That deception led to our enslavement to sin. Satan ruled us from the strongholds that he placed over our lives.

But God broke through enough strongholds to get us saved. So, now, we are tearing down the remaining strongholds that the devil has over our lives, and the lives of other people.

Tearing down strongholds is *offensive* warfare. We are capturing territory which used to be occupied by the enemy. We've already talked about defensive warfare—what we can do against the old tricks of the enemy. Now, it is time for Christians to go out on the offensive. *All of your life* has been claimed for Christ. So, don't let the devil rule any part of it.

Christian weapons are spiritual – weapons of the heart.

4. How did Jesus defeat the devil?

Then Jesus was led by the Spirit into the wilderness to be tempted there by the devil. For forty days and forty nights he fasted and became very hungry.
Matthew 4:1-2 (NLT)

Matthew 4:1-11 tells how Jesus was tempted by the devil. I find it a great comfort to know that we can defeat the devil in the same way that Jesus did.

The first thing you should know is that right before the temptation, Jesus received the anointing of the Holy Spirit in His baptism (Matthew 3:13-16; Isaiah 61:1). The Holy Spirit gave Jesus the power He needed to resist the devil's temptations.

It's very foolish to think that you can resist the devil in your own strength. **You need the Holy Spirit to help you**. That is because without the Holy Spirit, you have only the sinful nature which will undermine every attempt you make to resist temptation. So, when facing temptation, ask the Holy Spirit to help you fight temptation. He will help you every step of the way.

This brings up my second point in overcoming temptation. **Jesus fasted and prayed**. Prayer makes us stronger, when resisting temptation (Ephesians 6:18). It connects us to God and gives us access to His strength.

The devil couldn't deceive Jesus, because **Jesus knew the Bible**. Every time Satan tried to tempt Jesus, Jesus refuted the temptation with God's message. It's important to know that the devil knows the scriptures, too. He often tries to twist them, making them seem to say something that they don't. But Jesus was familiar with the whole Bible. That was how He defeated the devil.

Lastly, and most important, Jesus used **the authority in His name** to drive the devil away. Demons tremble at the name of Jesus. There is power in His name. The name of Jesus can drive out demons, heal bodies and restore lives (Mark 16:17-18). The name of Jesus can forgive all of our sins (Mark 2:10). That's because Jesus possesses all authority in heaven and on earth (Matthew 28:18).

Jesus has given you the right to use the authority in His name (Luke 12:31-32). So, if some annoying demon keeps "tempt, tempt, tempting" you, tell him where to go—in Jesus' name.

"Get out of here, Satan," Jesus told him. "For the Scriptures say, 'You must worship the LORD your God and serve only him.'"
Then the devil went away.
Matthew 4:10-11a (NLT)

---

1. Jesus relied on the power of the Holy Spirit
2. Jesus prayed and fasted.
3. Jesus knew the Bible.
4. Jesus used the authority in his name.

Review

1. Why does God call Christians Champions?

2. How do hardships affect our victory?

3. What types of weapons do Christians use against the devil?

4. How did Jesus defeat the devil during his forty days of fasting? (Four things)

Application

1. In this world, Christians are often looked upon as losers, because we don't compromise our integrity. We don't live like the people around us, because we are citizens of heaven (Philippians 1:27). We live under God's rule. What things do Christians do that are different from other people? Why do they do them?

2. We can follow Christ's example to defeat the devil. Can you think of anything Jesus did which helped him defeat the devil?

Prayer Time

Praise can sometimes be used as a weapon to defeat the devil. 2 Chronicles 20 tells a story about the Jewish King Jehoshaphat who destroyed an entire coalition of armies by praising God. Actually, God destroyed the coalition of armies, but it was Jehoshaphat's faith in God which brought God into action.

One of the most common ways for Satan to try to stop us from following Christ is by discouraging us. But praising God helps strengthen our spirits. It makes our faith stronger, more resolved to stand firm against any temptation.

So, while you are praying for Christ to help you and other Christians battling temptations, take time to praise Him for his many blessings and the victory He *will* give you, you mighty champion.

[For further study on spiritual warfare see the Armor of God, found in Ephesians 6:10-20.]

UNIT 7: CHRISTIAN LIVING

In this unit, we will explore how to apply our Christianity in our day-to-day living.

Lesson 1: Witnessing

1. What does it mean to love your neighbor?
2. Why is witnessing important?
3. What are three basic tools every Christian can use to lead others to Christ?

1. What does it mean to love your neighbor?

Do to others whatever you would like them to do to you. This is the essence of all that is taught in the law and the prophets.
Matthew 7:12 (NLT)

Most people have heard the story of the Good Samaritan found in Luke 10:30-37. The story is about a man who was traveling to another city when he stumbled upon a group the thieves. The thieves robbed him and beat him severely, leaving him to die along the side of the road.

A couple of clergymen came along the road, but when they each saw the poor man, they hurried away. Then a Samaritan (a social reject) came along. When he saw the desperate man, he stopped to take care of him. The Samaritan took the poor man to an inn where he recovered from his injuries.

Jesus told this story to answer the question, "Who is my neighbor?" found in verse 29. According to Leviticus 19:18, Moses told the Israelites to love your neighbor as yourself (NLT). Yet, the Israelites wondered, "Who does God require me to love?"

At the time of Jesus, Jews and Samaritans had been bitter enemies for hundreds of years (Ezra 4:1-5; John 4:9). However, both of these people groups had much in common. They both worshipped the same God (2 Kings 17:24-29). Both claimed to be descendants of Abraham (John 14:12). Both believed the Law of Moses was the word of God.

Of these two religions, it was the Jewish religion that was the most accurate (John 4:22). (At this time, Christianity was part of Judaism).

Yet, in this story, it was this Samaritan who actually *practiced* Christian love. Do you see the difference? Even though the clergymen claimed to obey God, it was this Samaritan who truly obeyed God.

Am I saying that it doesn't matter what a person believes? Of course not. Jesus plainly stated that He is the only way to the Father (John 14:6). However, Christians should be very careful the way they treat their so-called enemies. Jesus wants us to **treat others the way we want to be treated.** (Matthew 7:12) That is what it means to "love your neighbor."

Our real enemies are the devil and his demons, not the people of this world (Ephesians 6:10-12). So, treat your so-called enemies with love and kindness (Luke 6:27-28). Be good to them. If they are hurt, help them out (Romans 12:20-21). Don't give people an excuse to associate the name of Jesus Christ with anything evil (Matthew 5:13-15; 2 Peter 2:2; 1 Timothy 6:1).

2. Why is witnessing important?

Go into all the world and preach the Good News to everyone.
Mark 16:15 (NLT)

Let's pretend that a terrible disease has spread all across the world. This disease kills every single one of its victims. This disease is very contagious and it's a slow killer. So, it has plenty of

Treat others the way you want to be treated.

time to spread from person to person. It can even spread from parent to child.

Now, let's say that there is a cure for this disease and the best part is, you have the cure. A brilliant scientist has discovered a vaccine which completely cures any person who uses it and he has given this vaccine to you. So, you will live. You are now immune to the horrible disease.

So, you say to yourself, "Oh, how fortunate I am to have run into that scientist. He saved my life." Then you take the cure and you hide it away in a closet. You go on living your life, oblivious to the fact that billions of people are dying all around you.

The disease I am talking about is sin. Sin kills every one of its victims. The cure for sin is the Good News of Jesus Christ. We can be saved from our sins by trusting in Jesus Christ. The same Good News that saved you from your sins can save the person who lives right beside you (Romans 1:16).

But many times, we Christians are guilty of ignoring the person who lives beside us. Our neighbors go on sinning and dying just as they've always done. We go on ignoring their needs. We have taken the cure and hidden it in a closet and our negligence is killing them.

That's why I want to encourage you NOT to hide the cure in the closet. Let other people hear how they can be saved from sin and condemnation. Reach out to people by giving them the Good News. Sharing the Good News (or gospel) is what many Christians call "Witnessing."

I'm not saying that you have to save them. They have to want to be saved. You cannot save any person who does not want to be saved. But you do have a **responsibility to make sure that**

they at least *know how* to be saved (Acts 20:26-27). God will hold us accountable based on whether or not we tell other people about Jesus (James 4:17).

God sent his Son into the world not to judge the world, but to save the world through him.
John 3:17 (NLT)

3. What tools do we have to witness?

There are three important tools Christians have to witness to unbelievers. The most important tool you have is the Good News. **The Gospel (Good News)** is the death, burial and resurrection of Jesus Christ which saves us from our sins.

Put simply, all of us have sinned and deserve to die (Romans 3:23). But Jesus took our punishment by dying on the cross (2 Corinthians 5:21). Then He rose again so that we could have a new life in right standing before God. We receive this new life by trusting in Jesus for our salvation (Ephesians 2:8; John 3:16).

That's it. That is the gospel in a nutshell. Of course, the verse of scripture which also expresses the Gospel in a nutshell is John 3:16. Do you know it?

For God loved the world so much that he gave his one and only Son, so that everyone who believes in him will not perish but have eternal life.

John 3:16 (NLT)

So, if you at least know this much, you are equipped to tell others how to be saved. But there are two other important tools you can use to witness to unbelievers. One is with your **testimony**. Your testimony is the story of how you got saved.

Christians are responsible for making sure unbelievers know how to be saved.

Sharing your testimony helps you to relate to an unbeliever. It shows him or her that you are a *real human being.* You weren't born a saint. You've sinned and made mistakes, just like everybody else.

But most importantly, your testimony shows the unbeliever the difference Jesus Christ made in your life. Think about the sort of person you were like before you got saved and think about the type of person you are now. How has Jesus Christ changed your life?

Finally, the third tool you can use to lead people to Jesus is **setting a good example** for unbelievers (1 Peter 3:1-2). Whether you realize it or not, Jesus Christ is always on trial. People who don't know Jesus are always looking to see if Jesus really is as good as He claims to be.

The only problem is, they can't look into heaven to see what Jesus is *really* like. So, the only way they can tell whether or not Jesus really can transform an evil life into a good one is by watching you, the Christian.

They are watching you to see if you are sinning. This is a problem for many Christians, because it is very rare for a Christian to *never* sin. However, Christians don't claim to be perfect. What we claim is that Jesus Christ rescued us from being *slaves* to sin.

That's why if an unbeliever does notice you sinning, you should admit to it right away. Pretending that nothing happened will only cause them to think of you as a hypocrite and drive them further from Jesus Christ.

Setting a good example for unbelievers to follow isn't just about avoiding sin. Christians should be on the offensive. We can show unbelievers kindness. We can generously give them gifts. We can bless those who curse us. We can be cheerful in the worst of circumstances. We can love those who hate us and we can pray for them.

Tools for witnessing:
1. The Good News
2. Your Testimony
3. Setting a Good Example

UNASHAMED

I am convinced that we cannot successfully lead people to Christ without God's love. In the same way that love is the glue which keeps families together, love is vital to convincing people that our God is real.

One of the reasons why Christians don't witness to the lost, is because our love is lacking. Either we are short-tempered with people or perhaps it is because we are harboring pet sins. It's hard to witness to unbelievers if they can point out your most obvious sins.

I know what it's like to live with this kind of hypocrisy, because my sins used to keep me from telling others about Christ. But one day God showed me the attitude I had was wrong. God didn't want me to stop telling people about Jesus because of my sinning. He wanted me to stop sinning so that I can tell people about Jesus.

When I realized how my sins were harming the people around me, I knew I needed to stop. I had wanted to stop sinning before, but now I was determined to stop sinning.

Another reason why Christians don't share Jesus with others is because we are ashamed of Jesus Christ. Everybody wants to conform. We all want other people to like us. How can they like us if we are totally different? How can they accept us if we read our Bibles in the open or talk about Jesus freely as we would any other person?

I had this problem myself. I had a hard job where I worked nights and tried to sleep days and often between work and home, there just were not enough hours in the day to get my prayer and Bible time in.

Of course, I could do it in the workplace before I clocked in or on the bus ride going home, but that meant doing it out in the open.

Everybody would know I was a Christian then. I didn't want to be one of those crazy Christians. What if people found out I was a Christian, and later I sinned or made a mistake?

I tried over and over to get it done at home, but I kept falling asleep. But I wanted to read my Bible so badly. Finally, I could take it no more. I had to read my Bible and I didn't care if everybody knew about it.

I began reading my Bible daily at work and people quickly noticed that I was a Christian. But it no longer bothered me, because I was no longer ashamed of Christ. I became proud to be a Christian. I wound up having many opportunities to tell others about Christ.

I'll never forget what it was like when I finally let go of my fears. I cannot express the wonderful freedom and peace and joy that comes from living life unashamed.

Review

1. What does it mean to love your neighbor?

2. Why is witnessing important?

3. What are three basic tools every Christian can use to lead others to Christ?

Application

1. Think of the people either in your neighborhood, your school, work or in your family. Try to think of a few people to whom you could be a better neighbor. Who are those people? What can you do for them?

2. Do you know of anyone who is unsaved? Is there anyone who you are unsure whether or not he or she is saved? How can you know whether or not those people know how to be saved?

3. In which ways can you show a better example to unbelievers around you?

Prayer Time

As you pray, please focus on the people who need to hear God's message of salvation. Pray for them and pray for courage in overcoming your fears about sharing the Gospel. Ask God to help you witness to people, but don't let fear stop you from speaking to them.

Some people will hate you if you start asking them about salvation. That can't be helped. People don't like the pain dentists cause either, but we appreciate the fact that they save our teeth. A person's soul is much more valuable than his or her teeth.

So, pray for the people who need to be saved and pray that God will give you opportunities to share the Good News with them. I am certain that if you ask God to give you opportunities to witness that He will give them to you. Just make sure you take advantage of them.

Lesson 2: Christians at Work

In today's lesson we will explore how Christians should behave in the workplace.

1. Why should Christians work?
2. How should Christians work?
3. How should Christians share the Good News?

1. Why should Christians work?

Make it your goal to live a quiet life, minding your own business and working with your hands, just as we instructed you before. Then people who are not Christians will respect the way you live, and you will not need to depend on others.
1 Thessalonians 4:11-12 (NLT)

Which is a better way to live for God? To read the Bible and pray all day, every day or to spend some time in work or school?

Going to work is the better way to serve God. That is because there is a time for everything (Ecclesiastes 3:1). So, there is a time for reading the Bible and there is a time for going to work. The Christian life is balanced. It exhibits self-control.

Why should Christians work? We work **so that we don't become dependent** on others. If you don't work, you will wind up having to beg for money. Now, there are exceptions to this, especially in the case of those who are handicapped or orphaned—those who, for whatever legitimate reason, cannot work. This is what charitable giving is for (Galatians 2:9-10).

However, you don't want to be dependent on others, if you can help it. Being dependent on others puts you at their mercy and it gives them a degree of control over you. So, it's a healthy ambition to want to be able to fend for yourself, to be able to buy your own food and clothes.

Another reason why we work is to keep a good testimony in front of unbelievers. How do you think it looks for unbelievers to see Christians going around begging for money instead of working? It makes Christians look lazy and selfish.

Christians should be many things, but we should never be selfish. When Christians become selfish, no one cares to listen to the Good

Work so you won't become dependent on others.

News. That's because selfish Christians act nearly the same as people who don't even know God.

One final reason why Christians need to work is so that we can **support needy people** (Ephesians 4:28). As Christians, we don't just work for ourselves. We work so that we can help others around us who are in need and who, as mentioned earlier, are unable to work for themselves.

When we share with people who have legitimate needs, it gives us an opportunity to glorify God. Other people see that our generosity comes from God's work in our lives (Matthew 5:16). This encourages them to trust in God even more. Sometimes giving even creates an opportunity to share with others the Good News.

Even while we were with you, we gave you this command: Those unwilling to work will not get to eat.
2 Thessalonians 3:10 (NLT)

2. What should a Christian's attitude be towards a job?

Work with enthusiasm, as though you were working for the Lord rather than for people. Remember that the Lord will reward each one of us for the good we do, whether we are slaves or free.
Ephesians 6:7-8 (NLT)

These words were written by the Apostle Paul for Christian slaves, but I believe they apply to free workers, too. Have you ever felt unappreciated at your job? You come in each day and work hard and after it's all over no one even gives you a "thank you"? You take home the same meager income at the end of week. Then you go back to do it all again.

Work so you can support the needy.

Christians don't just work for money. For us, work is a form of worship. In the same way that praying or reading your Bible or giving to the church or serving other Christians are forms of worship, working is a form of worship, too. We work for God, not people. We are God's servants.

So don't get discouraged if you have a crummy boss. You don't work for your boss. You work for God. If you've been underpaid for all the good things you do, God sees it. On the Final Judgment Day, God will give you a fair reward.

But if you become embittered and you start shirking your work or vandalizing company property, God sees that, too. He will pay you back (Ephesians 6:25).

Of all people, Christians should never be lazy. If anything, we should be the hardest workers in the world. **We should do our best at what we do.**

So, don't just work. Get excited about working. See it as an opportunity to express your love for God. See it as an opportunity to earn a heavenly reward. See it as an opportunity to reach out to people in need. See it as an opportunity to help other people draw closer to God. See work as an opportunity to shine for Jesus.

3. How Can Christians Witness at Work?

Live wisely among those who are not believers, and make the most of every opportunity. Let your conversation be gracious and attractive so that you will have the right response for everyone.
Colossians 4:5-6 (NLT)

Whenever you work, you will most likely come in contact with other people. These other people might be your bosses, co-workers or even your customers. Some of them might be Christians. If they are, you can share with them what you know about God and encourage them.

> *Christians should do their best at what they do.*

Probably, many of the people you meet at work won't be saved. This is your opportunity to share with them the Good News. However, even in sharing the Good News, you should be careful how you do it, so that you don't give Jesus Christ a bad reputation.

Sometimes it's not best to share the Good News while in the act of working, because it might slow down or interrupt your work, making you look lazy. For some jobs, it might not matter, but for others, it would probably be best if you reserved your witnessing for off-hours, such as breaks or any extra time you have before or after your shift.

Another problem with witnessing happens when companies create rules against it. Some of these companies have very good intentions, although they are misguided.

Usually, the reason why companies create rules against witnessing is because an obnoxious Christian enters the company and tries to force people to get saved. He might be an overt person walking around yelling, "Repent! The Kingdom of Heaven is coming!" (Matthew 3:2) He might be an annoying Christian who keeps on nagging other people.

Christians who witness in a rude fashion mean well. They know the truth about salvation and they care enough to want other people to be saved. Yet, the way that they present the Good News only drives people away from salvation. And they give Christianity a bad reputation.

Take a moment and pretend that you are the unsaved person. How would you want Christians to present the Good News to you? Would rather they slam it in your face or would you prefer a gentler approach?

Many times, if you present the Good News to people in a gentle way, over a period of time it can win them over (Proverbs 25:15). In the end, **gentleness and patience** win the day. When you present the Good News in a harsh manner, it only makes them angry and drives them away (Proverbs 15:1). It's not enough for Christians to simply know the truth. We must also present the truth in a wise manner.

So, think of some gentler ways to let people know about Jesus. You might be able to place an appropriate tract or Bible verse pamphlet in one of the bathroom stalls. You might wear a cross pin. You might give a friend a gift with an invitation to church tucked inside it. You might exchange phone numbers with a co-worker and talk to him or her about Jesus outside of work. Many times, even saying a simple, "God bless you," is an appropriate way to witness to others.

In the same sense that there are many ways to praise God, there are also many ways to share God's love with other people. Try to find ways that respect other people and keep the peace in your workplace or school.

You're more likely to win a non-believer through gentleness and patience than by being harsh.

Review

1. Why should Christians work?

2. How should Christians work?

3. How should Christians share the Good News?

Application

1. What type of work do you do? Do you work your best?

2. How can you do a better job in your workplace or school?

3. What are some ways you can share the Good News with other people at your workplace or school?

Prayer Time

Today, pray for the people you work with. Pray for your co-workers and pray for your boss or bosses. Pray for any employees who work under you and pray for any regular customers you may have.

Are any of the people you work with unsaved? By all means pray for them. Are any of them facing a crisis? Pray for them. And there's nothing wrong with praying for your business to succeed or even flourish.

Employees should want their employers to flourish, because the more the company prospers, the more opportunities there will be for advancement (Genesis 39:2-5).

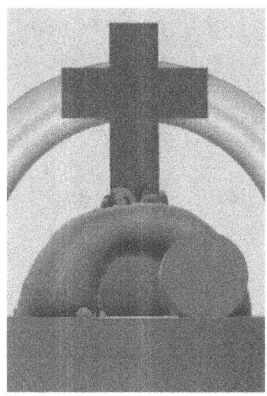

Lesson 3: Christians in Society

Christians live all over the world. So, we live under every type of government from religious to secular and democracies to dictatorships. How we live under those governments is important. In this chapter, we will discuss these questions:

1. What is the duty of a good government?
2. Why should Christians obey their governments?
3. How can Christians help to improve their government?
4. When must Christians disobey authorities?

1. Why do governments exist?

Everyone must submit to governing authorities. For all authority comes from God, and those in positions of authority have been placed there by God. So anyone who rebels against authority is

rebelling against what God has instituted, and they will be punished. For the authorities do not strike fear in people who are doing right, but in those who are doing wrong.
Romans 13:1-3a (NLT)

One of the main duties of good governments is that of punishing evil doers. Let me explain what I mean.

In any school there can be hundreds of different children all attending at the same time. Who keeps the stronger children from abusing the weaker children? It is the teachers who work at the school. What would happen if there were no teachers working at the school? The stronger children would abuse the weaker children and the weaker children would leave the school.

Governments offer us protection. If there was no government, society would be reduced to anarchy where only the strongest survive. How would you like to live in a world with sleepless nights, constantly looking over shoulder everywhere you go, terrified that someone might pull a gun on you at any moment? If there is no fear of government, that's the type of world we would all be living in.

But a good government punishes evil doers (Proverbs 16:12). They are the ones who say to abusers, "You can't do that." And they have police and military forces to reinforce their claims. When the government is enforcing the rules, people aren't afraid of getting their houses robbed or getting beaten down or killed. But when the government is weak or indifferent, people live in terror.

2. Why should Christians obey their governments?

So you must submit to them, not only to avoid punishment, but also to keep a clear conscience.
Romans 13:5 (NLT)

There are several reasons why Christians should obey government authorities. For one thing, governments aren't concerned with people who do good. They are only concerned with the people who are committing crimes.

It's kind of like the way it is in a school. In school, the best students are the ones who stay away from the principal's office. Why is that?

In any school, it's not the good students who get the principal's attention. It's the trouble-makers who concern the principal. The principal doesn't have to correct good students—they've already been corrected. Rather, the principal is trying to correct the evil students.

A good government punishes evil doers.

That's the way it is in society as well. **If you don't do anything wrong, then you don't have anything to be afraid of.**

Judges don't concern themselves with good people. It's the trouble-makers they want to correct. The best citizens are usually the ones who stay out of court (unless going to court is part of your job).

But there's another very important reason why Christians should obey government. How do you think it would appear if people in the government found out you were a Christian, but you were convicted of a crime?

Those government officials probably wouldn't want to become Christians, themselves. And why should they? If you claim to do good, but you're actually doing evil, then you've just put Christ's name to an open shame. Rather, we Christians should obey the laws of our country, so that **no government official will have anything to accuse Christianity of.**

> *If you don't do anything wrong, you shouldn't have anything to be afraid of.*

3. How can Christians improve their government?

> *I urge you, first of all, to pray for all people. Ask God to help them; intercede on their behalf, and give thanks for them. Pray this way for kings and all who are in authority so that we can live peaceful and quiet lives marked by godliness and dignity.*
>
> 1 Timothy 2:1-2 (NLT)

Christians should do more than simply obey the government. **We should pray for our government** as well. Every government has the potential to become good and every government has the potential to become evil. That's because every government is run by good or evil people.

> *Christians should obey their government so no official will have anything to accuse Christianity of.*

The battle for good government isn't just political—it's a spiritual battle as well. That's why we need to pray for our nation's leaders. If they are evil, pray that God will change their hearts. If they are good, pray that God will keep them firmly righteous.

Also, pray for the peace of your nation, and the best way for your nation to live in peace is if it becomes a good nation (Isaiah 48:22; 57:21). After all, how would you feel about a nation which started attacking other nations for no reason?

4. When must a Christian disobey?

But Peter and the apostles replied, "We must obey God rather than any human authority."
Acts 5:29 (NLT)

In general, Christians are required to obey all authority. However, sometimes Christians are required to disobey government authorities. When should you disobey a government? It is **when the government tries to get you to sin.**

If a government orders you to worship idols or false gods or tries to get you to stop meeting with other Christians or stop reading the Bible or stop praying or stop telling other people about Jesus Christ, then, of course, you should disobey.

> *One way Christians can improve their government is to pray for it.*

That does _not_ give you permission to try to overthrow your government. Christians are peacemakers, _not_ revolutionaries (Matthew 5:9; Proverbs 24:21). However, when human government challenges God's rule, God's rule is greater (Psalms 2).

There are several examples of believers who have challenged government authority. Elijah the prophet rebuked King Ahab (1 Kings 16:29-17:1). Daniel refused to eat King Nebuchadnezzar's food (Daniel 1:8). Shadrach, Meshach and Abednego refused to worship the king's idol. Peter and John refused to stop telling others about Jesus (Acts 4:16-22).

This puts Christians in a crisis, because human governments can imprison, torture and kill Christians. The first thing you should know is *your fate is not in human hands.* God often delivers His people from their enemies. Jesus passed through an angry crowd of Nazarenes (Luke 4:28-30). Peter was led out of prison by an angel (Acts 12:1-10). Daniel's friends were spared from the furnace (Daniel 3:24-29).

The second thing you should know is *there is a limit to what people can do to you*. The worst people can do is kill your body. Once your body is dead, there is nothing more they can do to you. Only God can kill your spirit. Only God can kill you, permanently (Matthew 10:28).

> *Christians should disobey the government when the government tries to make them sin.*

People may be able to imprison or torture you for a time. But sooner or later that time will end. That is nothing compared to the eternal imprisonment and torture waiting those who rebel against God (Revelation 21:8).

Dear friends, don't be afraid of those who want to kill your body; they cannot do any more to you after that. But I'll tell you whom to fear. Fear God, who has the power to kill you and then throw you into hell. Yes, he's the one to fear.
Luke 12:4-5 (NLT)

Review

1. What is the duty of a good government?

2. Why should Christians obey their governments? (Two things)

3. How can Christians help to improve their government?

4. When must Christians disobey authorities?

Application

1. Have you ever seen people who could not stay out of trouble, whether it was at school or in courts? What happens to people who are constantly getting into trouble?

2. How can Christians use good character to keep a good testimony in front of government officials?

3. Which people in government can you pray for today?

Prayer Time

Pray for your country, regardless of which country it is. There are many evil spirits trying to influence your nation's leaders, but God is trying to influence them, too. Pray that your nation's leaders would listen to God's influences instead.

Evil governments and even evil rulers can change their minds. King Manasseh was a mass murderer (2 Kings 21:16). He filled the streets of Jerusalem with the blood of innocent people. But when Manasseh was carried off to a Babylonian prison, he had a change of heart. He was released from prison and became a good king (2 Chronicles 33:1-13).

King Nebuchadnezzar desecrated God's temple (2 Kings 25:8-10). He encouraged idolatry and even tried to be a god (Daniel 3:4-5; 4:30). But when Nebuchadnezzar went insane for seven years, he became much more humbled. His kingdom was later restored to him and he gave God glory (Daniel 4:31-37). So, God can change evil governments (Proverbs 21:1).

EPILOGUE:

The Race

Forgetting the past and looking forward to what lies ahead, I press on to reach the end of the race and receive the heavenly prize for which God, through Christ Jesus, is calling us.
Philippians 3:13b-14 (NLT)

Think of a race. The gun fires. Every racer is out on the track, running hard. Each one is hurrying towards the finish line, hoping to finish the race and receive the prize that is waiting them.

One thing I have never noticed a racer do. I have never seen someone run a race, looking backwards. It is hard to run fast, if you're always thinking about what is going on behind you.

The Christian life is a lot like a race. Like runners in a race, we should always run our race looking forwards, not backwards.

Forget the past. Who you used to be is dead. You don't have to wallow in the shame of lost promises and lost time. Today is a new beginning and you are God's new creation.

Instead, look to the future, the distant future. Look all the way to the end of the race, the end of your life here on earth. There God is waiting for you with arms wide open and a heavenly reward.

In God's race, it's not the fastest person who wins the prize. It is the person who is faithful. It is the person who runs the entire distance.

It's easy to want to give up. It's easy to say to yourself, "Forget this. I'm too tired. I don't want to run anymore." It's easy to want to walk right off the track, go back to that easy sinful way you used to live.

You know who the people are who give up on Jesus Christ. They are the people who keep looking back. They keep trying to run forward, looking back at their old pet sins, and wishing somehow that the race wasn't so difficult.

But you won't have to worry about looking back, if your eyes are fixed on Jesus. Jesus *is* the end of your race. To be with Jesus is your destiny. To rule with Jesus is your prize.

So, keep on running. Keep looking forward and run your race all the way through. God is with you.

And let us run with endurance the race God has set before us. We do this by keeping our eyes on Jesus, the champion who initiates and perfects our faith.
Hebrews 12:1b-2a (NLT)

RESOURCES

I have put together a group of resources to help new Christians grow in their faith in God. I have arranged these resources as follows.

Resource 1: Reviewing
Review Questions
Review Answers

Resource 2: Bible Tools
I. How to Get a Bible
II. Finding Scriptures
III. How the Bible is Organized.
IV. Bible Study Tools

Resource 3: Church Tools
I. How to Find a Church
II. Selecting a Church

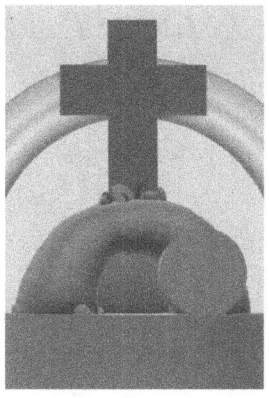

Resource 1: Reviewing

Have you ever enjoyed reading a book only to discover that about a month after you finished reading it, you forgot all about it? That's what these review questions are designed to help you with. They are designed to **help you remember** the things you learned while reading this book.

I have included two sections in the Reviewing Resource. The first section, Questions, is designed to simply show you all of the questions in the book. The second section, Answers, allows you to see the answers to each of the questions.

I encourage you to use these two sections to quiz yourself to see how much you can remember. First read the question by itself. Then try to answer it. Finally, check to see if you answered it correctly. If you keep doing that over and over, you will find that you can remember a great deal.

I. QUESTIONS

UNIT 1. THE GOOD NEWS

Lesson 1: Where Did I Come From?

1. How did God create humanity?
2. What is God's view of humanity, today?
3. What is the punishment for sin? (Two things)
4. What is the Good News?

Lesson 2: How Do I Become Saved?

1. How do we become saved? (Two things)
2. How does God save us from sin?
3. What is becoming a Christian like?
4. What are the benefits of becoming a Christian? (Four things)

Lesson 3: Where Are We Going?

1. What will happen after a Christian dies?
2. Why should Christians live to please God?
3. What does God offer us in eternity? (Three things)

UNIT 2. GOD

Lesson 1: Who is God?

1. Who is the Godhead?
2. Who is God, the Father?

3. Who is God, the Son?
4. Who is the Holy Spirit?

Lesson 2: Who is Jesus Christ?
1. What Does Jesus Christ Mean?
2. What Makes Jesus Human?
3. What Makes Jesus Divine?
4. What is Jesus doing for us today? (Two things)

Lesson 3: What is God Like?
1. How do God's ways compare with our ways?
2. What are God's ways (Seven characteristics)?

UNIT 3. DEVOTIONS

Lesson 1: Prayer
1. What is prayer?
2. Why shouldn't you worry about your problems?
3. How should you pray to God?
4. What should we do if God doesn't answer right away?
5. What should we do when God answers our prayers?

Lesson 2: Bible
1. Why do we read and meditate on the Bible? (Two things)
2. Why do we study the Bible?
3. How does memorizing the Bible help us? (Two things)

4. What happens when we don't obey the Bible?

Lesson 3: Praise

1. What does praise do for us?
2. What makes praise a sacrifice?
3. Why should we praise God in hardships?

UNIT 4. THE CHURCH

Lesson 1: God's Family

1. What is the family of God? (Three things)
2. Where did the church come from? (Three things)
3. Why is church attendance important?

Lesson 2: Baptism and the Lord's Supper

1. What is water baptism?
2. What does baptism mean?
3. What is the Lord's Supper?
4. What is Lord's Supper supposed to do for us?

Lesson 3: Giving and Service

1. Why should Christians give? (Three things)
2. How should Christians give? (Two things)
3. Why are some Christians different from others?
4. How should Christians use spiritual gifts?

UNIT 5. SANCTIFICATION

Lesson 1: The Sinful Nature
1. Why can't Christians use God's grace as an excuse to sin? (Three things)
2. Why can't people please by obeying God's laws?
3. How does a Christian mature?

Lesson 2: Following the Holy Spirit
1. How do we identify the sinful nature?
2. What are the nine fruit of the Spirit?
3. What is the goal of holiness?

Lesson 3: Personal Convictions
1. How do we live among Christians with different personal convictions than us?
2. What do I do if I have a sensitive conscience? (Two things)
3. What do I do if I have a relaxed conscience? (Two things)

UNIT 6. SPIRITUAL WARFARE

Lesson 1: The Enemy
1. Who is our enemy?
2. What are demons?
3. What is Satan's destiny?
4. How can a Christian prepare against Satan? (Three things)

Lesson 2: The Devil's Schemes

1. What are trials?
2. What do hardships do for Christians?
3. Why are Christians persecuted?
4. How does Satan introduce deception to the church?

Lesson 3: God's Mighty Champions!

1. Why does God call Christians Champions?
2. How do hardships affect our victory?
3. What types of weapons do Christians use against the devil?
4. How did Jesus defeat the devil during his forty days of fasting? (Four things)

UNIT 7. CHRISTIAN LIVING

Lesson 1: Witnessing

1. What does it mean to love your neighbor?
2. Why is witnessing important?
3. What are three basic tools every Christian can use to lead others to Christ?

Lesson 2: Christians at Work

1. Why should Christians work?
2. How should Christians work?
3. How can Christians witness at work?

Lesson 3: Christians in Society

1. What is the duty of a good government?
2. Why should Christians obey their governments? (Two things)
3. How can Christians help to improve their government?
4. When must Christians disobey authorities?

II. ANSWERS

UNIT 1. THE GOOD NEWS

Lesson 1: Where Did I Come From?

1. How did God create humanity?
   - We were originally good.
2. What is God's view of humanity, today?
   - God sees us as evil people.
3. What is the punishment for sin? (Two things)
   - Death. Ultimately, an everlasting torment.
4. What is the Good News?
   - The death, burial, and resurrection of Jesus Christ, which saves us from our sins.

Lesson 2: How Do I Become Saved?

1. How do we become saved? (Two things)
   - Confess that Jesus is Lord and believe that God has raised Him back to life.
2. How does God save us from sin?

- God's grace through our faith.

3. What is becoming a Christian like?
   - We become a new creation.

4. What are the benefits of becoming a Christian? (Four Things)
   - God declares us righteous, we are at peace with God, we have His favor, and we have a glorious future waiting us.

Lesson 3: Where Are We Going?

1. What will happen after a Christian dies?
   - We will come back to life when Jesus returns.

2. Why should Christians live to please God?
   - Christ will one day judge us.

3. What does God offer us in eternity? (Three things)
   - A new paradise. An eternal home. God will be with us.

UNIT 2. GOD

Lesson 1: Who is God?

1. Who is the Godhead?
   - The Godhead is one God in three persons: the Father, the Son, and the Holy Spirit.

2. Who is God, the Father?
   - God who is in heaven and rules over all things.

3. Who is God, the Son?
   - Jesus Christ, who lived with us and died to save us from our sins.

4. Who is the Holy Spirit?
- God who lives within us and helps us to live godly lives.

Lesson 2: Who is Jesus Christ?

1. What Does Jesus Christ Mean?
- Jesus means Savior, Christ means Anointed One.
2. What Makes Jesus Human?
- He was born, had parents, had an ethnic group, had a body, ate, drank, slept, was tempted and died. The only difference between Jesus and us is Jesus never sinned.
3. What Makes Jesus Divine?
- Jesus always existed. He created all things, claimed to be God, performed countless miracles, and resurrected Himself.
4. What is Jesus doing for us today? (Two things)
- Jesus continues to represent us to the Father and He is preparing a special place for us in the New Jerusalem.

Lesson 3: What is God Like?

1. How do God's ways compare with our ways?
- God's ways are higher than our ways.
2. What are God's ways (Seven characteristics)?
- God is compassionate, merciful, patient, loving, faithful, forgiving, and just.

UNIT 3. DEVOTIONS

Lesson 1: Prayer

1. What is prayer?
   - Requests made to God.
2. Why shouldn't you worry about your problems?
   - God already knows about your problems.
3. How should you pray to God?
   - Believe that God wants to give you good gifts.
4. What should we do if God doesn't answer right away?
   - Keep on asking.
5. What should we do when God answers our prayers?
   - Thank God.

Lesson 2: Bible

1. Why do we read and meditate on the Bible? (Two things)
   - God's word can save our lives from sin and teach us to live wisely.
2. Why do we study the Bible?
   - Bible studies help us to understand the Bible more completely.
3. How does memorizing the Bible help us? (Two things)
   - Bible memorization helps us understand what God wants and keeps us living a righteous life.

4. What happens when we don't obey the Bible?
- We deceive ourselves into thinking we are good, when we really are not.

Lesson 3: Praise

1. What does praise do for us?
- It strengthens our faith.
2. What makes praise a sacrifice?
- It helps us develop a humble attitude.
3. Why should we praise God in hardships?
- That is when our faith is really really being tested.

UNIT 4. THE CHURCH

Lesson 1: God's Family

1. What is the family of God? (Three things)
- The Father, Jesus Christ, and us (adopted by the Holy Spirit)
2. Where did the church come from? (Three things)
- Jesus, the apostles and NT prophets.
3. Why is church attendance important?
- Christians draw strength from each other.

Lesson 2: Baptism and the Lord's Supper

1. What is water baptism?

- A Christian rite that involves dipping or washing a Christian with water.

2. What does water baptism mean?
    - Water baptism symbolizes repentance—to turn from sinful living towards God.

3. What is the Lord's Supper?
    - The Lord's Supper is a form of worship where we eat bread and wine to remember Jesus Christ's death on the cross.

4. What is Lords Supper supposed to do for us?
    - The Lord's Supper is supposed to bring Christians together.

Lesson 3: Giving and Service

1. Why should Christians give? (Three things)
    - Giving offers protection against tragedy, the opportunity to bless others, and a way to enrich your life.

2. How should Christians give? (Two things)
    - Give in proportion to what you have. Give cheerfully.

3. Why are some Christians different from others?
    - God has a different purpose for each Christian.

4. How should Christians use spiritual gifts?
    - Christians should use their gifts to show God's love to others.

UNIT 5. SANCTIFICATION

Lesson 1: The Sinful Nature

1. Why can't Christians use God's grace as an excuse to sin? (Three things)
   - We are dead to sin. So we don't become re-enslaved to sin. Sin leads to death.
2. Why can't people please God by obeying God's laws?
   - Without Christ we are already slaves to sin, because of our sinful nature.
3. How does a Christian mature?
   - By following the Holy Spirit

Lesson 2: Following the Holy Spirit

1. How do we identify the sinful nature?
   - The sinful nature tends to lead us towards selfish and out of control thinking.
2. What are the nine fruit of the Spirit?
   - Love, Joy, Peace, Patience, Kindness, Goodness, Faithfulness, Humbleness, and Self-Control.
3. What is the goal of holiness?
   - To become like Jesus Christ.

Lesson 3: Personal Convictions

1. How do we live among Christians with different personal convictions than us?

    - Accept other Christians who have different convictions.

2. What do I do if I have a sensitive conscience? (Two things)

    - Know what your personal convictions are, and don't budge from them.
    - Don't condemn another Christian whose personal convictions are different.

3. What do I do if I have a relaxed conscience? (Two things)

    - Don't get mad at the person who has a sensitive conscience.
    - Be considerate of other Christians needs so you don't tempt them.

UNIT 6. SPIRITUAL WARFARE

Lesson 1: The Enemy

1. Who is our enemy?

    - Satan, also called The Devil and Prince of Demons.

2. What are demons?

    - They are evil angels (evil spirit beings).

3. What is Satan's destiny?

    - Eternal torment in the Lake of Fire.

4. How can a Christian prepare against Satan? (Three things)

    - Be aware of the devil's schemes.

- Watch out for the devil.
- Resist the devil.

Lesson 2: The Devil's Schemes

1. What are trials?
   - Anything which tests our faithfulness to God
2. What do hardships do for Christians?
   - They bring us closer to Christ, if we have the right attitude.
3. Why are Christians persecuted?
   - Unbelievers envy Christians, because Christianity exposes sin.
4. How does Satan introduce deception to the church?
   - From immoral messengers

Lesson 3: God's Mighty Champions!

1. Why does God call Christians Champions?
   - Because we are defeating the world by our faith.
2. How do hardships affect our victory?
   - Hardships affirm that we are champions.
3. What types of weapons do Christians use against the devil?
   - Spiritual weapons—weapons of the heart.
4. How did Jesus defeat the devil during his forty days of fasting? (Four things)
   - Jesus relied upon the Holy Spirits anointing.
   - He fasted and prayed.

- He was familiar with the Bible.
- He used the authority found in his name.

UNIT 7. CHRISTIAN LIVING

Lesson 1: Witnessing

1. What does it mean to love your neighbor?
    - Treat other people the way you want to be treated.
2. Why is witnessing important?
    - Christians are responsible for making sure unbelievers know how to be saved.
3. What are three basic tools every Christian can use to lead others to Christ?
    - The Gospel (Good News). Your testimony (how you got saved).
    - Setting a good example (because you love Jesus).

Lesson 2: Christians at Work

1. Why should Christians work?
    - So we won't be dependent upon other people.
    - So we can support the needy.
2. How should Christians work?
    - We should do our best at what we do.
3. How should Christians share the Good News?
    - With gentleness and patience.

Lesson 3: Christians in Society

1. What is the duty of a good government?
   - To punish evil doers.
2. Why should Christians obey their governments? (Two things)
   - If you do good, you have no need to fear the government.
   - To keep a good Christian testimony in front of government officials.
3. How can Christians help to improve their government?
   - Pray for your government.
4. When must Christians disobey authorities?
   - When those authorities require Christians to sin.

Resource 2: Bible Tools

I. HOW TO GET A BIBLE

If you don't have a Bible on hand there are several ways you can get your hands on one—some of them are free.

1. Buy a Bible in a Bookstore or a Bible Bookstore. This is probably the most obvious way to get a Bible. It is the way most people get Bibles, because it is the most convenient.

2. Buy a Bible in a Used Bookstore or Thrift Store. Most cities and some towns have used book stores. Most are locally owned although some are owned by charitable organizations. Usually, you can get Bibles much cheaper in these second-hand stores, but they might not always have Bibles available. If they do have Bibles, they might not be the exact type that you're looking for.

3. Get a Bible from a church. Several large churches run into problems when the janitors or custodians keep finding lost Bibles lying around in church. People take their Bibles to church, but forget to bring them home. Many times, the people who own these lost Bibles never come back to church to claim them. They simply go out and buy another Bible. You can check with the church offices to see if they have any extra Bibles that had been sitting around for a long time.

4. Ask a fellow Christian for a Bible. Many Christians don't have one Bible, but dozens of Bibles lying around the house. So, it's likely that you could find a Christian who would give you one, if you need one and are willing to ask.

5. Borrow a Bible from the library or from the Internet. If all else fails, try the library or the Internet. Every library carries copies of the Bible which can be borrowed if you have a library card. Whether or not they have type you're looking for often depends on how large the library you're visiting is. You may also be able to find copies of the Bible or Bible software on the Internet.

II. FINDING SCRIPTURES

A. Basics to Referencing Scripture

Referencing Scripture is one of the most important skills any Bible student can learn. If you have ever seen a scripture reference, such as Matthew 7:12, it can seem daunting at first until you understand it better.

In our sample reference, Matthew 7:12, the word Matthew refers to the Book of Matthew, which is found in the Bible. The Book portion in a Bible reference can refer to one out of 66 books of the Bible. You can find them in the Table of Contents page, towards the very front of your Bible.

The Table of Contents page lists all of the books of the Bible and gives the page numbers to help you find each book in the Bible. For example, your Table of Contents might say that Matthew is on page 1107. So, if it does, you simply turn to page 1107 in your Bible and you should be able to find the very beginning of the Book of Matthew. Most likely, your Bible's Table of Contents will have a different page number. But this is your first step towards finding the scripture Matthew 7:12.

The numbers in a Bible reference refer to the chapter and verse numbers of the scripture. The number on the left of the colon (:) is the chapter and the number to the right is your verse. So, in our sample reference, Matthew 7:12, the number 7 refers to chapter seven and the number 12 refers to verse 12. Here it is:

Do to others whatever you would like them to do to you. This is the essence of all that is taught in the law and the prophets.
Matthew 7:12 (NLT)

See if you can find this verse in your Bible. Depending on your Bible, it might be worded slightly different, but the meaning of this verse will be the same. As long as you remember the basic format (Book Chapter : Verse), you should have no serious difficulty finding specific verses in scripture.

B. Complications in Referencing Scripture

Before I close this segment on referencing scripture, I want to mention some of the more complicated aspects of scripture referencing. For example, instead of seeing Matthew 7:12, you might see Matthew 7:12-13 or Matthew 7:12, 13. All this means is that there is more than one verse in the Bible reference.

You might also see multiple verses referenced in different chapters of the same book, such as (Matthew 5:43; 19:19; 22:39). This refers to the verses Matthew 5:43, Matthew 19:19, and Matthew 22:39. All three of the verses tell us to love our neighbors.

You might see Matthew 7:13a or Matthew 7:13b. What this means is that only part of the verse is being referenced. The "a" refers to the beginning of a verse and the "b" refers to the ending of a verse.

You might see a reference that says, Matt. 7:12 instead of Matthew 7:12. Matt. is nothing more than an abbreviation for Matthew. So, you might see Lev. instead of Leviticus or Prov. instead of Proverbs. Don't let that throw you off.

You might see a number in front of the book, instead of behind it, such as 2 Corinthians 5:17. In the Bible, there are two books named Corinthians. They are First Corinthians and Second Corinthians, or 1 Corinthians and 2 Corinthians.

1 & 2 Corinthians are tricky books for any new Bible student to reference. The reason why is because they look very much like two Old Testament Books (1 & 2 Chronicles). These four books look even more similar when they are abbreviated: (1 & 2 Cor.) vs. (1 & 2 Chr.)

Another tricky book to reference is John, or St. John which refers to the Gospel of John, the fourth book of the New Testament. If you see 1 John, it is referring to the First Letter of John, which is found shortly before Revelation, at the end of Bible.

Also Philippians and Philemon look the same when they are abbreviated (Phil.), but Philemon is seldom referenced and only has one chapter. So, if you see a scripture like Phil. 2:5, you know it is referring to Philippians, not Philemon.

Aside from these tricky books, most other books in the Bible are easy to reference. I hope you have fun finding scriptures with your newly acquired skill.

III. HOW THE BIBLE IS ORGANIZED

If you take a look in your Bible's Table of Contents at the front, you will see a listing of 66 books. (There are more books if your

Bible has an Apocrypha/Deuterocanon Section). At first glance the arrangement of the books will likely seem haphazard, but there is a reason why they are arranged the way they are.

Most Bible have two sections of books—The Old Testament (OT) and the New Testament (NT). The Old Testament covers the time period from Adam to just after the Jewish exile. The New Testament covers the lives of Jesus and the Apostles, satisfying the requirements of the Old Testament.

Each Testament is further divided according to its literature types.
- Old Testament - The Law, History, Poetry, Prophets.
- New Testament - The Gospels, History, Letters, Prophecy.

This is the arrangement of the **Old Testament** books.

The Law is the first five books of the Bible (Genesis, Exodus, Leviticus, Numbers, and Deuteronomy). These books are accredited to Moses who delivered God's commandments to the Israelites.

History is the Books of Joshua through Nehemiah. The history begins with the Conquest of Canaan, tells the stories of the judges, the kings, the prophets and ends with the return of the Israelites from exile. These books provide a historical backdrop for poetry and prophecy of scripture.

Poetry is Job, Psalms, Proverbs, Ecclesiastes, and Song of Solomon. These books are full of poems and songs expressing great emotion, wisdom and even prophecy.

The Prophets includes the *Major Prophets* (Isaiah-Daniel) and the *Minor Prophets* (Hosea-Malachi). The prophets were God's messengers to Israel. Often they corrected the Israelites sins, but they also encouraged the Israelites, as well. Many of the prophets looked ahead towards the coming of a future Jewish King.

This is the arrangement of the **New Testament** books.

The Gospels includes Matthew, Mark, Luke, and John. They tell us the Good News of the ministry of Jesus Christ from his baptism to his death, burial, resurrection and ascension. They show us how Jesus is the coming king foretold by the OT prophets.

History is the Book of Acts. It lists the actions of the Holy Spirit through the apostles, spreading the Good News throughout the world from Jerusalem to Rome. The Acts provides the historical backdrop to understanding the Letters of the Bible.

Letters (*Epistles*) is divided into two groups. *Paul's Letters* are all the books from Romans to Philemon. They are accredited to the Apostle Paul. The *General Letters* were written by the other apostles and include the books Hebrews to Jude. In their letters, the apostles teach Christians how to live a godly life.

Prophecy is the Book of Revelation, which is almost entirely end-times prophecy. The Book of Revelation covers everything from the Great Tribulation to the Great White Throne Judgment and the New Jerusalem, bringing the Bible to a conclusion.

If you take the time to explore the Bible in further detail, you will gradually begin to understand some of the mysteries of the Bible. For example, who wrote the Book of Proverbs? Why are some books divided? What is an acrostic psalm? What languages were the Bible originally written in? Why does the NT quote the OT so often? Why does the Bible end with Revelation? I hope you have fun exploring the Bible.

IV. BIBLE STUDY TOOLS

Below I have listed a wide variety of study tools which you might find useful for exploring the Bible.

Bible Handbooks are designed to introduce the reader to the Bible. They present an overview of the Bible by giving historical background about the Bible as well as the Bible's main divisions (i.e. Old Testament, Law, History, Poetry. . .).

Then they take each book of the Bible and offer historical background as well as outlines. Handbooks are best for first time Bible readers, but can be useful references for experienced Bible students as well.

Bible Dictionaries are probably the most indispensable Bible tool. They help you find information about a wide variety of bible-related topics. For example, Bible dictionaries help us to define specific biblical terms such as covenant or baptism. They also offer a rich amount of historical information. You can find summaries about people, places, or events in the Bible and even learn about the History of the Bible.

Concordances are designed to show us where we can find specific words within the Bible. If you ever wondered where in the Bible the word believe is found, you can simply look the word up within the concordance.

Although good concordances are nearly indispensable, they do have their limitations. One of the problems with concordances is that each Bible translation requires a different concordance. Also, most concordances help you find *words* in a Bible, not topics or phrases.

Lexicons - Lexicon is another word for dictionary. The main difference between a lexicon and a Bible Dictionary is that a lexicon is a dictionary of another language, not biblical terms. Take the word lord, for example. The Greek language has more than one word for lord. Lexicons help Bible students to understand the exact meaning or the full meaning of a word or phrase used.

They are also useful for familiarizing yourself with the original Bible languages.

Commentaries are tools where someone else has done the Bible study for you and is giving you his or her understanding of it. Commentaries vary widely. Some focus mostly upon practical application of the Bible while others focus mostly upon historical background or understanding of the Bible.

Parallel Translations - The Bible has been written in a variety of translations. A parallel translation tries to take two Bible translations and arrange them side by side so that you can easily see how each translation is rendered.

The main advantage a Parallel Bible offers is that it is a lot easier and quicker to look up the passage in a Parallel Bible than it is to look that same passage up in two separate translations, particularly if they are two translations of the Bible that you tend to use often. Some Parallel Translations offer the Bible in other languages for people who are trying to learn a foreign language.

Study Bibles - A study Bible is usually designed to give the reader the best of a wide variety of tools. They usually have book introductions, chain references, maps, time lines, and commentaries, etc. It's like having a Bible, Bible Dictionary, Handbook, Commentary, and Concordance all rolled up into one.

Although Study Bibles cost more than ordinary Bibles, the value of a good study Bible often far outweighs that cost.

Bible Software is the most efficient way to study the Bible. It usually offers several translations, which you can view simultaneously. Looking up a scripture has never been easier. Simply type in the reference or click on the link.

Bible Software packages offer search engines which not only allow you to look up words, but also phrases or parts of words. Often they have Greek and Hebrew lexicons in them. Some even offer Bible dictionaries, commentaries, handbooks and maps.

Bible Software packages vary widely in both their prices and in their abilities. They don't really offer any new study tools that you can't use a book for. But what they do, they do fast. It is many times faster to click on a link than it is to flip through several pages of text.

Resource 3: Church Tools

One of the first things many new Christians have a hard time doing is finding and choosing a church to go to. Of course, you could simply choose a new church to attend each week, but if you do that you won't develop any real relationships with any other Christians. In order to get to know other Christians it's important to keep attending the same church.

I. HOW TO FIND A CHURCH

1. Ask Christian friends to recommend a church. This is a great way to find a new church fast and you have someone to tell you what the church is like without ever having to visit.

2. Find a church within the phone book or internet listings. Just look up the word "churches" in the yellow pages or on or on its website. You can find names, numbers, addresses and even maps to the churches on the internet listings. Unfortunately, you won't get much information on what the church is like.

3. Read your newspaper. Many newspapers post church advertisements for Christians looking for churches in their weekend listings. It's not as exhaustive as the yellow pages, but you can get a slightly better idea of what some of the churches are like before visiting them.

II. SELECTING A CHURCH

There is no criteria listed in the Bible for selecting a church and no church is perfect. However, you may find these suggestions helpful.

1. Find a church that preaches the Bible.

When you listen to the minister preaching, think about what he or she is saying. Many of the things a minister preaches might or might not be true. How can you know for certain?

The way you find out is by comparing what the minister says to the scripture. Is the message this person speaking in agreement with what the Bible says?

If what the preacher say agrees with scripture, then you know he or she is a trustworthy preacher. However, if the preacher often ignores or contradicts the Bible, you should probably stay away from that church.

2. Find a church where the congregants love each other.

Another thing that I would look for within a church congregation, is a church family that loves each other. If you're visiting a church, take a moment to look at how the members of the congregation treat each other. Do they treat each other warmly as brothers and sisters or do they seem to be trying to avoid each other? Does everyone in the congregation receive respect, or is there favoritism in the church?

If I were visiting a church, I wouldn't judge that church by how friendly they were towards me personally, because nobody in that church really knows me yet. I haven't had time to develop any type of relationship with them. But if the people in a church love each other, then there's a very good chance that they will love you as well, once they get to know you.

Don't forget that it's important for you to show love to the church you are visiting, too. So, when you're visiting a church, don't just sit there like a stone statue, hoping and praying that someone will come and talk to you. Take the initiative. Get out of your seat, go up to some of them and shake hands. You'll be glad you did.

www.ingramcontent.com/pod-product-compliance
Lightning Source LLC
Chambersburg PA
CBHW070536010526
44118CB00012B/1141